MANAGING PERFORMANCE MANAGING PEOPLE

MANAGING PERFORMANCE
MANAGING PEOPLE

Understanding and improving team performance

Murray Ainsworth

Neville Smith

Anne Millership

Pearson Education Australia
Unit 4, Level 2
14 Aquatic Drive
Frenchs Forest NSW 2086

Publisher: Nella Soeterboek
Commissioning Editor: Mark Stafford
Project Editor: Jane Roy
Copy Editor: Janice Keynton
Indexer: Jo Rudd
Cover and internal design: DiZign Pty Ltd
Typeset by Midland Typesetters, Maryborough Vic.

Printed in Australia by Griffin Press

1 2 3 4 5 06 05 04 03

National Library of Australia
Cataloguing-in-Publication Data

Ainsworth, W.M. (W.Murray).
    Managing performance, managing people: understanding and
    improving team performance.

    Bibliography.
    Includes index.
    ISBN 1 74009 616 9

    1. Personnel management. 2. Teams in the workplace.
    I. Smith, Neville, I. II. Millership, Anne. III. Title.

658.402

An imprint of Pearson Education Australia

Contents

Preface

This book is intended as a practical guide for managers. It will help them to explain the performance levels of their people, whether high or low. It will allow them to diagnose causes underlying performance issues. It will also enable them to manage the key factors which influence job performance.

All concepts are presented in everyday language; you'll find little jargon and no heavy theoretical discussion. However, be assured that there is a body of respectable research and knowledge behind the concepts presented in this book.

Over the last six or seven decades much has been learned and written about people at work. Managing, motivation, goal setting, individual needs, incentives, leadership, job design, supervision, participation, conflict and competencies are just some of the topics that have been explored. Theories abound. So much has been written, debated, researched and written again that many managers find it hard to know where to start.

That's where this book comes in. It provides a simple and useable framework which brings together much of what is known and presents it in a form which managers can use on a day-to-day basis.

It is a book about building individual and team performance by managing better. And it describes how to do just that.

The key performance factors, which are the focus of this book, are presented in the form of a 'performance model'. A variation of this model is also presented in the form of a performance 'equation'. This is an original way of portraying the interaction of these factors. Each chapter from Chapter 4 onwards explores one of these factors. These chapters are in two parts: the first part explains the factor and how it influences performance; the second explores what managers can do to manage that factor. The final chapters examine the skills, mostly those of verbal communication, which underpin effective performance management.

A list of relevant further reading is provided at the end of the book.

Chapter 1

Introduction — performance and people

Tom Burns is a member of the Hot Shots, a local basketball team. They are playing the Bombers, and the score is 56–42 in favour of the Bombers. Things are not going well for Tom Burns and the Hot Shots.

The coach, Mike, calls time-out. He gathers the team around him and says:

Mike: What's going wrong?

Tom: Well . . . I'm not getting into the guard position very well.

Boyd: We're just not clicking.

Third player: They're really hot.

Mike: Well, we need to get out there and show our stuff. Tom . . . you're off. Bill, take over from Tom. The rest of you . . . get out there and shoot some baskets. There's a bonus in it for tonight's game.

The Hot Shots lose. Tom, a little depressed, approaches Mike:

Tom: Why did you drop me?

Mike: You weren't playing well.

Tom: I tried to tell you, I'm uncomfortable at guard. But I've been in form as a forward.

Mike: Look, Tom, this is a team game. You've got to be flexible to support the team.

Tom: Yes . . . but it might have made a big difference to the team's result if I'd been playing where I could contribute.

Mike: Perhaps . . . but the game's over now.

Doesn't it make you wonder? How often are the causes of performance shortfalls assumed, rather than explored? Mike, the coach, assumes everyone simply needs some stimulation, some incentive. But is that really the case? Let's ask Boyd, the player who said 'We're just not clicking'.

Interviewer: Boyd, what did you mean by your comment?

Boyd: Well, I don't want to point the finger, but Tom was out of position a lot. I couldn't find him when I needed him.

Interviewer: Is he usually a bad player?

Boyd: Hang on, that's not what I said. Tom's usually a good player . . . reliable hands, good passer, everything you could ask for. He was just in the wrong place too much tonight.

Interviewer: Would you have dropped him?

Boyd: No . . . I would have moved him to forward. He's too good a player to go without.

Interviewer: So you feel you know better than the coach?

Boyd: This is off the record?

Interviewer: Yes.

> **Boyd:** The coach should have tried running Tom at guard during training, to give him a better understanding of that position. He just didn't know what to do when playing at guard. It's not Tom's fault.

Does this story reflect the way things are sometimes managed where you work? Is this how the question of 'performance' is addressed in your work groups, departments, sections or teams? Are performance problems diagnosed with hunches and managed with snap decisions? Have you got a Mike, a Boyd or a Tom on your team? Some team member who is under-utilised, under-skilled, simply in the wrong role or position?

This is a book about managing more effectively. It's about how to manage the performance of your own group (including yourself). It is immaterial whether the setting is in manufacturing, finance, e-business, government, statutory bodies, education or other service sectors. The success of the organisation – and of you – the manager, is determined by how well the collective performance is managed.

Performance is the key. If you are a manager it is what you are paid for. It is your primary responsibility: producing outcomes (performance) from your team by using all the resources possessed by or accessible to them.

This book's objectives are to help managers to:

● understand the causes of performance,

● diagnose performance shortfalls, and

● manage performance to the desired level.

The word 'performance' should be well fixed in your mind by now. It has already been used 12 times in this chapter. But what does it mean?

Basically, it means an outcome – a result. It is the end point of people, resources and certain environments being brought together, with the intention of producing certain things, whether a tangible product or less tangible service. To the extent that this interaction results in an outcome of the desired level and quality, at agreed cost levels, performance will be judged as satisfactory, good, or perhaps even excellent. To the extent that the outcome is disappointing, for whatever reason, performance will be judged as poor or deficient.

Rather than become greatly concerned at this stage with definitions, it is more useful to consider the factors affecting people's performance at work.

The simplest explanation says individual performance is a function of ability and motivation. That is, it is the outcome of:

being able to (ability) (A) × wanting to (motivation) (M)

So

Performance = A × M

Given a moment's reflection, however, this appears inadequate. For instance, what about the tools available? If they're not appropriate, 'ability' cannot be effectively used. The best salesperson in the company will soon perform poorly with an unreliable car and a faulty phone! No matter how hard they want to win the 'Top Sales Performer of the Year' award, their environment may be such that they can't achieve better than mediocre results.

What about the systems in place to support the person? Are they adequate? How good is the database management? And what about a real understanding of the task? The most able person, highly motivated but poorly instructed or directed, is not going to perform well except by chance, which raises the quality of leadership as another factor.

Clearly, there's more to it than just $A \times M$. This is just too simple an approach. Some other attempts, however, go too far in the opposite direction. These over-complicate performance by listing every major and minor issue that may be relevant. One model identifies 40 such factors operating at six different levels. While that might be a nice exercise in academic rigour, it is of little assistance to the practising manager. It avoids the 'too simple' criticism, but opens itself up to another one – too complex! Forty factors cannot be kept at the front of one's mind! It is just too much, and too complicated.

As a practical guide for use by those who are out there managing, something more valid than the first simplistic model, but more useable than the second (40 factor) model, is required. And that's what this book provides (see Chapter 2).

Performance management

The term 'performance management' can be used in more than one way. To some, it refers to the performance of the organisation. In such cases, it covers the planning concepts of vision, mission specification, strategy development and specification of goals and objectives. It also includes measuring the achievements of the organisation against the stated goals.

To others, performance management refers to individuals or small teams at work. In such cases, it also covers planning, but planning for the person or the group. These plans are, of course, part of the larger organisational plan. There is also measurement, often called appraisal. But there is also diagnosis and help for the individual or the small group to develop. This is shown in Figure 1.1.

Figure 1.1 Performance management

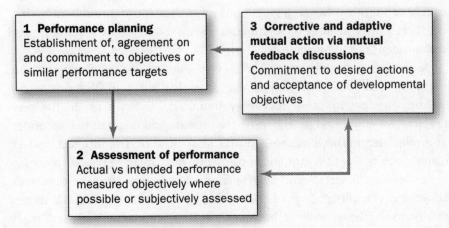

1 **Performance planning**
Establishment of, agreement on and commitment to objectives or similar performance targets

3 **Corrective and adaptive mutual action via mutual feedback discussions**
Commitment to desired actions and acceptance of developmental objectives

2 **Assessment of performance**
Actual vs intended performance measured objectively where possible or subjectively assessed

This book deals with the second approach, that is, performance of individuals and small groups. It assumes that the important corporate issues of 'mission' and goal setting have been addressed and resolved. It assumes that objectives for the sub-sections of the organisation (the departments, divisions or business units) have been set within the key results areas, and that the senior management group has identified just where the competitive advantage and value-adding dimensions of the business lie. It further assumes that all of this has been communicated to and understood by those involved in the performance management process outlined in Figure 1.1; hopefully, they have been involved in at least some of the decisions!

Figure 1.2 provides an overview of performance management. This is one way of viewing the relationship between the type of performance management dealt with in this book and the broader meaning of performance management at the corporate or divisional level. There are many other ways of representing this relationship. The shaded box at the bottom of Figure 1.2 indicates where this book fits into the big picture of organisational performance.

A major reason for 'performance management' breaking down at the individual or small group level is that the boss and their team members simply don't 'talk it through' adequately. And 'talking it through' at each of the three stages outlined in Figure 1.1 is essential if some understanding and commitment are to be achieved.

Managers generally don't find interactions to do with performance planning (see box 1 in Figure 1.1) too difficult and those who are uncomfortable with face-to-face discussion revert to simply asking the team member for suggested objectives (or whatever) to be submitted on paper. The manager makes changes and returns these as the 'agreed' list. Of course, commitment is not confronted, but normal hierarchical pressures are usually sufficient to ensure some degree of acceptance of the objectives. Unfortunately, generating a performance plan in this way usually means clarifying the 'how much' rather than the 'how'. Questions such as 'How to

Figure 1.2 Performance, and this book

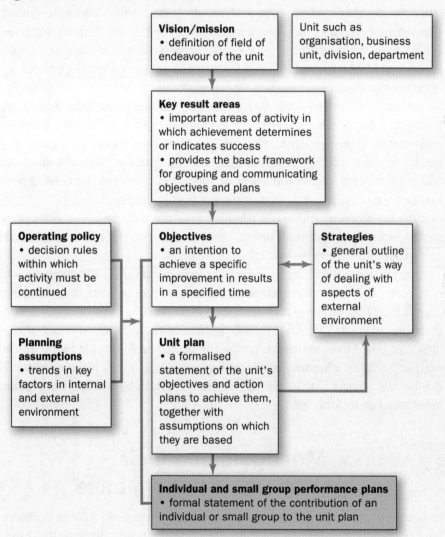

work?', 'How to change?', 'How to assess?', 'How to cope?', 'How to succeed?', 'How to develop?' remain unaddressed. Increasingly, computer-based systems are being used in performance management, but that in itself does not change the underlying process. Sometimes, the fact that seemingly sophisticated systems can be run at a distance works against the overriding need for discussion, agreement and commitment.

Interactions to do with performance measurement (see box 2 in Figure 1.1) and feedback (see box 3 in Figure 1.1) supposedly take place at some sort of review session and it is difficult to see how these can be anything but face-to-face sessions, regardless of how the data has been obtained. At this stage a very high proportion of individuals in organisations report ineffective discussions with their supervisors or managers.

Why are so many managers unable to handle performance feedback in a developmental manner, even though they consider they conduct 'appraisal interviews'?

One reason is that they lack the interpersonal skills for conducting such a discussion. A more fundamental reason, however, is that they have no overall frame of reference for such a discussion and no clear understanding of the major factors which influence performance. This was a cause of the difficulty that Mike, the coach of the Hot Shots, had with his team. There was no sensible diagnosis and discussion of the performance shortfall (losing the game). Mike just did not know what he should have been monitoring or looking for.

Managers and their expectations of performance

In a republished article in the *Harvard Business Review*, Robert Schaffer (1991) suggests that most managers don't hold sufficiently high expectations of their people's performance potential.

This may or may not be true. What perhaps can be argued more strongly is that managers don't *convey* high performance expectations to their people. There are doubtless many reasons for this. Our Australian tradition of egalitarianism is one reason. If John or Margaret is as good as his or her master, then the master is not too keen on making it clear that a good deal more is expected of them. For some managers the Industrial Relations culture will reinforce this view: high expectations may be seen as 'impossible' because of union and labour force attitudes supported by employment contracts. Other reasons may be to do with the managerial culture ('We've been doing okay as we are – let's not rock the boat'), because the significant gains which a new manager might be able to achieve would make the predecessor and the present boss look poor. And who wants to take that risk and then live with the consequences? Managerial colleagues may also resist new performance standards, which might expose their own anxieties and behaviour. The thought of failure is also a disincentive. If we do raise performance expectations and then fail to achieve these new goals, what will we have to do to 'fix it'? Maybe we would have to get *really* tough, or let people go, or worse – bring in consultants! The anticipated consequences of failure are a powerful deterrent to risk-taking, as is the thought of rejection by the team if they are asked for too much.

All of this helps to explain why managers may be unaware of the gap between the performance they at present require, and what might actually be possible. Relying on existing goals and procedures just looks a lot easier!

Next season, when Mike is familiar with the performance factors in the following chapters, he will have the Hot Shots playing at the top of the ladder. He will have learnt to use the factors to:

- explain the performance of team members and diagnose apparent difficulties
- provide a structure for performance counselling and coaching
- agree to contracts for improvement with players

When Mike returns to his weekday job he will also be likely to view work and people at work in a developmental way.

If Mike works his way through this book carefully, he will have a solid frame of reference at his disposal, and some tools for using in future discussions with his team.

Chapter 2

A performance model

If managing performance is a vital part of managing, and it surely must be, then understanding and explaining performance is a responsibility of every manager. But this is easier said than done.

Performance is a difficult word. It is even difficult to define. Are the outcomes (the result) of a group's effort always a reasonable indicator of the group's performance? Normally, yes. But not always. For example:

- A mining group's output can vary sharply as ore concentrations change even though constant effort is applied continuously. In this case, the constraint on performance is quite outside the control of those involved.

- A building materials sales group will find output decreasing (lower sales) during a downturn in the building industry. This macro-economic factor is outside the control of the manufacturer, and extra effort at the team level is unlikely to compensate.

- Restaurateurs found business very poor on the opening night of the Sydney Olympics (very few people went out), even though their effort and resourcing was normal.

Performance concepts appear to be primarily differentiated by how the performance is measured. *'If it can't be measured, it can't be managed'* is a frequently heard refrain.

For example, highly quantitative measures give productivity indices often expressed as ratios of output per applied resource. Others employ two-factor scales, results and effort, even though the 'effort' element is judged quite subjectively. A popular and much-used approach, with its origins back in the 'management by objectives' school of thought, requires consideration of the following factors:

- Key result areas/key objectives
  - the areas of responsibility, or objectives in which required outcomes are to be defined
- Key tasks
  - the major tasks for each key result area or objective
- Performance measures (or key performance indicators)
  - what will be measured, and how, so that performance or 'success' can be confirmed
- Performance standards
  - how many of the chosen factors must be achieved and to what standard

In such approaches, the measures would normally focus on:

- Productivity – considering measures such as volume, throughput
- Costs – human, processing and raw materials
- Quality – acceptability, closeness to specification, reject rate, standards met
- Customer satisfaction – number of complaints and compliments, level of satisfaction

● Timeliness – meeting agreed deadlines and schedules

Not everyone is attracted to the rigour and discipline of this approach (nor do all work settings allow sufficiently tight measurement) and hence some managers are quite content with qualitative judgments of 'performance' as distinct from outcomes and productivity measures.

Performance at work – the factors involved

Irrespective of the measurement details, there is little doubt that a number of factors affect how well an individual, or a team, works. And it is likely that pursuing these factors provides a way of understanding performance that is not constrained by unrealistic measures and definitions.

Let us make this clear by working through an example. Let's suppose you have hired us to landscape your yard. You know in advance that we are not experienced gardeners or landscapers, so you will need to manage us closely. You start this process by giving clear instructions:

> *Today I want you to terrace this backyard, from here to here, building two retaining walls here and here.*

When you return, you see the yard neatly terraced. It looks great. But your neighbour is complaining that his yard is subsiding. (Apparently we dug out some of the support for his yard that is uphill from yours). You ask us,

> *Didn't you leave retaining protection on his side?*

and we of course reply,

> *Did you want us to?*

Our performance is unsatisfactory, as we didn't know that shoring-up or stabilising was part of the role we had taken on. Nor did we know that keeping the relationship with the neighbour intact was part of our role, albeit unspoken. Clearly, role clarity, as well as many other things can affect performance.

If we call performance P, role clarity Rc and all other factors affecting our performance the unknown x, then we see that

Performance (P) is a function of
Role clarity (Rc), and
Some additional unknown factor(s) (x).

For those readers who like equations think of it as:

$$P = Rc \times x$$

At this stage, you have identified a lack of role clarity as part of the explanation for our poor landscaping performance. But you'd be wise to keep exploring. Clearly x can be broken apart – it's not much use having an unknown!

Suppose when you returned you found the terracing quite uneven. You complained. We responded:

'I'm sorry. We've tried and tried. That's the best we can do.'

Clearly, if we don't have competence to do a job, then there's very little chance of it being done well. If we call competence C, then

Performance (P) is a function of
Role clarity (Rc) and
Competence (C), and
the unknown x factor.

$$P = Rc \times C \times x$$

You've now identified two factors very relevant to our performance. That's surely an adequate explanation, so you can go off to work the next day believing all will now be well with the landscaping job.

Then . . . you return and find that we have barely started. We have sweated and sweated with two small spades. You rightly ask,

> 'Is that all you've done?'

And we respond indignantly,

> 'No one could have done more with this equipment! We haven't even
> got a decent shovel or a crowbar; this equipment you've given us is
> hopeless.'

Clearly, outcomes are affected by the adequacy of tools. In fact, there's a total environment in which the work is taking place, in which equipment is only one element. If we call this E for environment, then our definition grows.

Performance (P) is a function of
Role clarity (Rc) and
Competence (C) and
Environment (E) and
the unknown x factor.

$$P = Rc \times C \times E \times x$$

Note that this environment factor includes more than just 'tools'. If the neighbour had become abusive and threatened us, we may have said 'this is an awful place to work' and gone home early with the job quite neglected. Clearly there is a human or 'social' dimension to the work environment as well. Alternatively, if you had come home early and negotiated with the neighbour so that our work could continue thanks to your provision of such leadership, then that human dimension would have been reflected in a different way.

This, and other components of the 'environment' will be discussed in Chapter 6.

So you, the manager of your landscaping project, have yet another factor to manage.

And so to a different scenario. You return once more and find yet again that almost no work has been done. You demand to know why. We inform you there are several rare trees in your yard and we've sent for a ranger to find safe ways of removing them. You are quite upset at this delay for what you consider trivial reasons, but we are convinced this is an important issue. Our value system is in conflict with yours and, of course, ours will not permit us to proceed, so performance is affected. So we can recognise another part of x: V for values. So, the growing relationship becomes:

Performance (P) is a function of
Role clarity (Rc) and
Competence (C) and
Environment (E) and
Values (V) and
the unknown x factor.
$$P = Rc \times C \times E \times V \times x$$

Now, what if you came back and the job was half done. There are two of us, and one has dug and shifted quite well but the other has become preoccupied taking plant cuttings. You call aside the one who has been working and say,

'What's with that other person? Is he lazy?'

The reply is

'No, he doesn't like this type of work we are doing today: but I do.
We're a team. There are other things I don't like where he does more
than his share. So, we get on okay. We share it out.'

Clearly, what an individual likes to do affects their performance. We call this idea preference fit or Pf; the degree to which the individual's preferences fit with the job.

Performance (P) is a function of
Role clarity (Rc) and

Competence (*C*) and

Environment (*E*) and

Values (*V*) and

Preferences (*Pf*) and

the unknown *x* factor.

$$P = Rc \times C \times E \times V \times Pf \times x$$

Of course, you had better promise to pay us enough to make it worth our while to labour over your yard. If you don't fail to let us know of the potential reward before we begin, you might come back to an untouched yard. Rewards clearly affect performance and rewards are only effective if they are appropriate to the motives of the people concerned. So, in our case, dollar payment would probably be appropriate!

If you're astute, of course, you might realise that we would also see recognising our concern for the rare trees as a 'reward'. You may even decide to let us keep them! That is the kind of reward that might result in us starting work early tomorrow and going through until the job is complete! We would see you as a manager who understood our point of view – even though you might not agree with it. Adding this to our considerations,

Performance (*P*) is a function of

Role clarity (*Rc*) and

Competence (*C*) and

Environment (*E*) and

Values (*V*) and

Preferences (*Pf*) and

Rewards (*Rw*)

$$P = Rc \times C \times E \times V \times Pf \times Rw$$

There may well be other components of *x* remaining. But our experience tells us these are either difficult to define and apply (such as temperament) or impractical to manage (such as the external environment to which the employee belongs, primarily family and friends). So, for ease of use, and our practical objectives, we have now eliminated our 'unknown' *x* factor, leaving performance determined by the six factors above.

While this list is relatively comprehensive, it doesn't emphasise the simple fact that if any one of these factors is reduced to zero, then performance is zero (or almost). For example, if we have no skills at all related to landscaping, then we simply couldn't start the job. Or if we thought the rewards inadequate (close to 'zero' in our minds) then we either wouldn't take on the job, or if we did the quality would be highly suspect, even assuming we turned up on the first day!

So a basic message is that each factor

● is important, and

● needs to be managed

if the landscaping job is to be completed successfully.

Values

The values factor seems to work differently from all the other factors. It is virtually 'all on' if the task is right or okay and there is no 'conflict of values', and 'all off' if the task is seen to be in conflict with the values held by the individual or work group. But it's not just a simple 'on' or 'off' condition: there are 'grey area' jobs which people will do without trying very hard, a sort of 0.5 or 0.6 effort. And if economic need is truly paramount then some people will significantly sacrifice their values to feed their family. But the 'on or off' nature of values suggests they act as a gateway to the other personalised factors (preference and rewards). We need to remember that these three attitudinal factors – values, preferences and rewards – can, on occasion, be dominated by the values issue.

Some simple examples of how values can override other considerations follow.

If I am offered the job of smuggling drugs, do I take it ? It is a good fit with my preferences (I like travel to foreign places, and often to off-the-beaten-track locations, as well as meeting new and different people), and the rewards are very good (all expenses paid, and lots of money on return . . .) but do I take the job? Most of us say 'No' as our values tell us that this is not an activity we can support, let alone become directly involved in. Our values override the individual activities that we would otherwise find attractive.

Does the social worker seek work with the city-based consultancy that works mostly with stressed senior executives? (Her counselling skills fit her to be competent in the job.) Probably not. Her values (belief in the importance of helping the truly disadvantaged) may override her preferences (working with people) and the rewards (better salary in the consultancy).

Because values can impact so adversely on performance, it is placed outside parentheses to show that it can pre-empt or overrule the other attitudinal factors, preferences and rewards. So the whole factor is expressed as

$$V (Pf \times Rw).$$

The performance model

The full performance model now comprises:

P Performance Defined and measured in appropriate ways. Is it P = Productivity (quantifiable) or is it P = Performance (qualitative judgment) or is it P = Perhaps (highly subjective judgment)?

Rc Role clarity How well do people, singly and collectively, know what is expected of them? How well do they know how they fit into the bigger picture?

C Competence Do people have the knowledge and skills to do what is expected? What likely deficiencies are there? What skills and knowledge are needed today? What will be needed in the future?

E	**Environment**	Three elements must be conducive to doing the things required:

- The physical environment – the tools and the workplace physical conditions
- The human environment – group factors such as compatibility, team cohesiveness and the vital leadership factor
- The organisation – clarity of structure, systems, communication of priorities and emphases, and workplace culture

V	**Values**	Do people generally accept that what they're asked to do and what the organisation does, is not wrong? (This is probably a 'negator' of performance rather than a multiplier.)

Pf	**Preference fit**	Are people generally in jobs containing activities they like? The degree to which an individual's preferences and the demands of the job fit together seems to affect the following:

- Job satisfaction
- Time management – both in terms of discretionary time and particular bias to tasks
- Preparedness to work outside normal hours (when relevant)
- Retention of talent

Rw	**Reward**	Are people rewarded appropriately according to their expectations, their performance, their individual motives and their need for feedback? Rewards may be either:

- Explicit (things the manager or organisation gives or says) or
- Intrinsic to the work (directly rewarding the individual's motives)

Later chapters of this book will more fully explain each of these variables plus the concept of feedback.

Clearly, these variables differ in significance from one organisation to the next. Some organisations are somewhat bureaucratic, with role clarity and competence emphasised but with common reward systems across whole classes of employees (that is, low emphasis on reward). Others are overtly entrepreneurial, emphasising individual freedom (probably via flexibility over preferences – *'We'll try and arrange for you to mostly do what you enjoy . . .'*) and results-based compensation (a highly variable reward, related more to individual contributions).

If there is too great a bias either way (that is, too much emphasis towards role clarity and competence, or too much towards preferences and rewards) it may cause performance problems. These will require management to review the underlying strategies. This is not the field of the performance model, or of this book. In practice, we've found the model to be useful primarily when looking at individual and/or small group performance.

How can the model be used?

A reasonable question at this time is 'How is the model used?' Over the past several years we've seen a vast volume of literature presenting interesting models which explain performance at various levels of complexity. What is usually missing are ideas about using these frameworks. We will not make that mistake here. As well as the suggestions that follow, you will find a series of illustrations throughout this book which demonstrate the use of the model.

We use the model in our work as a diagnostic tool. We don't see it as a precise mathematical arrangement, but rather as a mental map or checklist to help us find out what is wrong, what is right and what is going on in a particular situation.

Essentially it provides factors for discussion in any performance-focused conversation. Diagnosis will be part of that discussion.

But diagnosis is for a purpose: to correct, or to bring back on course. And correction implies discussion and feedback. Feedback on both outcomes and behaviour is, of course, a vital factor: and ideally is two-way. It provides a link to all other factors through dialogue between managers and employees, and so feedback is the final component of the model. This is illustrated as follows:

PERFORMANCE is a function of
ROLE CLARITY and
COMPETENCE and
ENVIRONMENT and
VALUES and
PREFERENCES and
REWARDS plus
FEEDBACK

The factors in this model provide a frame of reference that will assist you to manage a wide range of performance situations. The model can be applied to:

● *Modifying and enriching jobs.* It is usually easier to modify a job than to force change on a person. This is acknowledged when jobs are designed to broaden responsibilities, improve work practices and provide individuals with improved satisfaction and rewards. This typically involves specification of roles, acquisition of competence and improvements to work environments, including restructured work groups (to change the human dimensions of the environment). The increased frequency of multi-skilling as a work practice is an example of job enrichment through broadening the competency base.

- *Creating new and improved skills.* There is marked interest in the community in upgrading competencies across a wide range of industrial and commercial activities, including managerial work. This is true for both the public and the private sector. This typically involves the following factors represented in the model: competence, preference and rewards.

- *Improving communications.* Using the factors in the model, feedback will become more focused and is more likely to be two-way and more specific. Improved feedback means improved communication between a manager and the team member. There will also be opportunities for self-assessment and developmental activities using the model as a framework.

- *Career development.* There is implicit acceptance of the importance of human differences and the right of individuals to strive for careers that fit their preferences. This is acknowledged in the restructuring of employment contracts, where developing a career path is seen as an important part of the work contract. Developing career paths requires attention to role clarity (present and future), competence (to be developed) and preferences (for better job satisfaction). Clarification of likely future rewards will also be necessary.

- *Change management.* The pressures for change are now commonly felt throughout industrial, commercial and service organisations. The model as presented provides a structure by which individuals can look at the implications of a planned change. A shift in position, a change in reporting relationships, or an organisational restructure can affect any or all of the performance factors.

- *New reward structures.* Increasingly, reward systems which acknowledge improved contribution are being established as part of enterprise agreements and employment contracts. This includes the idea of rewards for new competencies, which may be accepted as an industry-wide requirement. This clearly involves both competency and reward factors from the model.

To check out your understanding of this chapter and to become comfortable with the factors and the use of diagnosis which the factors allow, look seriously at your own performance. There's a reasonable chance that shortfalls can be found. Admit to them. List the factors and ask these key questions:

Role clarity	Do I know precisely what is expected of me? Do I know how what I do contributes to the total picture?
Competence	Do I have skills, knowledge and aptitude appropriate to the tasks I'm expected to do?
Environment	Do I have all the tools and equipment I need to work well? Do I have an effective work group and systems? How do I rate the leadership?
Values	Do I think that all we do is 'not wrong'?
Preference	Do I like all activities in my work? (Are there other things I'd rather be doing?)
Reward	Do I feel adequately rewarded, both in my pocket and in my heart, at the end of the day?

An alternative expression of the model

As has been shown on the previous pages, we have often found it useful to introduce groups to these same performance concepts through the use of

a performance equation

It is simply the same factors presented in a visually different way. The scene has already been set for this, because each factor has been represented by a symbol: P for Performance, Rc for Role Clarity, C for Competence, Pf for Preference Fit, etc. So it is not a big jump to put them into the form of an equation. We have found this useful in a training situation (introducing managers and supervisors to the performance factors), where a group of participants can be involved in building the 'Equation' and exploring the implications.

The equation can be built, through discussion with the group, a factor at a time, so that it finally looks like Figure 2.1 below.

The factors detailed above will be followed by another factor –

Private life/personal matters

to acknowledge the reality which we all know . . . that frequently life outside work impacts on life inside work, and that only a foolish manager or supervisor would pretend that was not so.

The equation also makes clear through its mathematical expression several important points:

- The multiplication signs imply that if any factor is zero, the performance will be zero.
- Without taking the above point completely literally, the implication for the manager is that ALL those factors need to be managed.

Is it any wonder we all go home tired some days? There is a lot there to be aware of, and to be managed!

Figure 2.1 The performance equation

$$\textbf{Performance} = \textit{Rc} \times \textit{C} \times \textit{E} \times \textit{V} (\textit{Pf} \times \textit{Rw})$$

plus

FEEDBACK

Chapter 3

Performance management systems – an organisational context

The last several decades have seen organisations giving increased attention to performance management. The objective has been to develop performance management systems that focus on optimising employee's performance and their potential. Why is this? Because organisations, whether they are private companies, public bodies or small businesses, regard the process of performance management as a practical and mostly effective way to address human resource and productivity issues.

The fact is that people want to know what to do in their job and how to do it. Increasingly, organisations are developing performance management systems to help meet these needs through clarifying goals and monitoring progress. Indeed, people want to know more – they want to know what is expected of them, how they are progressing, what their manager or boss thinks of their performance and generally where they fit into the organisation, both now and in the future. A well-designed performance management system should address all these needs and concerns of employees.

Successful organisations in Australia and overseas have in place performance management systems that are 'integrated': that is, they effectively link individual performance with corporate strategy. The fundamental elements of these integrated systems are:

- the identification and communication of the organisation's strategic goals,
- the translation of strategic goals into business unit and departmental goals, and
- their application at the team and individual levels.

Both the team and the individual can therefore see how their jobs and their efforts contribute to the overall performance and achievements of the organisation. These elements provide the framework for

- the cascading of goals and objectives through the organisation,
- the setting of performance targets, and
- the review of achievement against these agreed objectives for employees at all levels in the organisations.

Link with corporate strategy

The fundamental aim of a performance management system is to improve organisational, team and individual performance. The model below (in Figure 3.1) illustrates how an organisation can link its corporate strategy to individual objectives through its performance management system. If you read any literature on performance management, you will find many versions of this model. Basically they are all the same – they include the same essential elements and provide a framework that links each element.

Figure 3.1

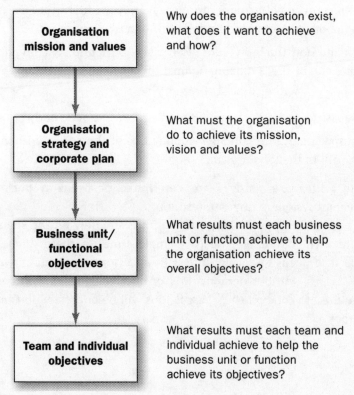

Organisation mission and values	Why does the organisation exist, what does it want to achieve and how?
Organisation strategy and corporate plan	What must the organisation do to achieve its mission, vision and values?
Business unit/ functional objectives	What results must each business unit or function achieve to help the organisation achieve its overall objectives?
Team and individual objectives	What results must each team and individual achieve to help the business unit or function achieve its objectives?

But what is often implied but not identified in these models, is the alignment with the corporate planning cycle. That is, setting annual corporate performance targets (including financial plans) and aligning with them many individual plans. Furthermore, the timing of these processes is critical – one should follow the other, within a relatively short time span. If a team or an individual is to have relevant, current and therefore meaningful performance targets, these targets must come directly from the current corporate plan. And so the time between finalising the annual corporate plan and the setting of team and individual targets must be as short as possible.

But linking and aligning individual performance to corporate strategy and setting agreed performance targets are only the first steps. The next and equally important steps are to decide through discussion:

- when and how the individual receives feedback and coaching about progress he or she is making against these targets,
- how these targets are reviewed,
- what assistance he or she needs to meet these targets, and
- what specific training and development he or she needs, both in the short and in the longer term.

These issues are really what can make or break a performance management system in any organisation.

The responsibility of making this work sits squarely on the shoulders of each manager. A manager needs to make time for these discussions. A manager also needs to develop the skills necessary to enable discussion of sensitive issues, without demotivating or alienating team members. (The skills required to conduct these discussions will be addressed in Chapter 11 of this book.)

Performance management

A critical issue for any manager is recognising good and bad performance and responding appropriately. For some managers, the issue lies in awareness, or the ability to identify and acknowledge a performance issue when it arises. For other managers, the issue lies in responding to a performance issue, in both a timely and an effective way. For others still, the issue lies in being objective, rather than subjective, when evaluating an individual's performance. Following a systematic approach to managing performance can assist in addressing these matters.

Figure 3.2 describes performance management as a systematic, four-step process that managers could follow when managing the performance of any individual or team.

The process of performance management includes the four steps of:

1. Performance planning – setting and agreeing goals and targets.

2. Regular performance review and discussion – reviewing progress against goals and targets.

3. Performance evaluation – measuring and evaluating performance against goals and targets and identifying and verifying gaps in performance.

4. Corrective and adaptive action – developing strategies to close performance gaps.

Step 1 – performance planning

Logically, the first step should be driven directly by the business unit in keeping with the corporate goals and objectives, as discussed above. Without this step, either the manager or the individual may not agree or commit to what needs to be done, by when and by whom. A collaborative effort of the manager and the individual will produce goals and targets that should be recorded and used as the basis for further discussion throughout

Figure 3.2 The performance management cycle

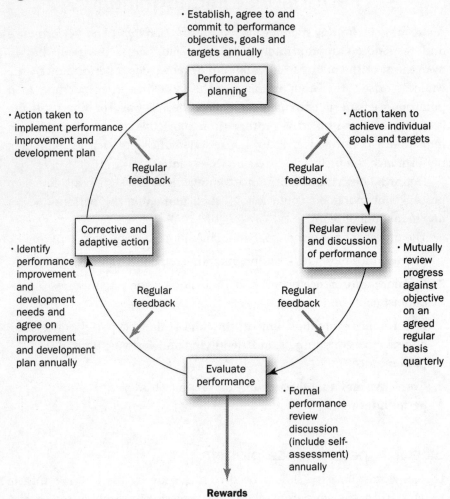

· Establish, agree to and commit to performance objectives, goals and targets annually

Performance planning

· Action taken to implement performance improvement and development plan

· Action taken to achieve individual goals and targets

Regular feedback

Regular feedback

Corrective and adaptive action

Regular review and discussion of performance

· Identify performance improvement and development needs and agree on improvement and development plan annually

· Mutually review progress against objective on an agreed regular basis quarterly

Regular feedback

Regular feedback

Evaluate performance

· Formal performance review discussion (include self-assessment) annually

Rewards

the period. This record becomes the tool by which both the manager and individual can gauge progress and performance.

But it not always easy to define specific goals nor to actually measure their achievement. As mentioned in Chapter 2, not every job or workplace is easily suited to the rigour and discipline of quantitative goal-setting and measurement, as originally defined in the MBO (Management by Objectives) approach. Nor are all managers or individuals comfortable with purely quantitative goals and measures – they also like to consider more qualitative goals and measures of performance which can be observed rather than measured. The challenge, however, is to make these goals and measures as objective as possible and to minimise subjectivity.

After David finalised his business plan for the unit for the next 12 months, he had it approved by his General Manager. His next step was to meet with each of his team members to develop their goals and targets for the next 12 months. He decided to give each team member a copy of the business unit plan and ask them to think about how it related to their own job, and then to draft some goals and targets for themselves for the next 12 months. He would then meet with each team member individually to discuss their ideas and agree on what each individual had to achieve to ensure the business unit plan was met.

Step 2 – regular performance review and discussion

During the year, after setting and agreeing goals and targets, it makes common sense for the manager and the individual to meet to discuss the individual's progress against their goals and targets. The performance plan forms the basis of this discussion. The review meeting:

- provides the opportunity to identify what obstacles are getting in the way of the individual achieving their goals,
- helps identify what additional help or support they may need,
- enables the parties to check if the previously agreed goals and targets are still relevant or need some adjustment (for example, because

business priorities or other things have changed since the plan was agreed).

Some organisations formalise this step in their performance management systems. They do this to ensure that these reviews and discussions occur regularly, for example quarterly or every six months, and that these discussions are fully documented for later reference and use.

David was able to agree on goals and targets with each of his team members within a month of finalising his unit's business plan for the next 12 months. Generally, the team members said that they preferred having regular fortnightly meetings with David and all members of the team to receive feedback on how the unit is progressing and whether it is on target to achieve its goals and targets. The team also wanted the opportunity to raise, discuss and hopefully resolve any problems or issues the team is having. But this was not enough. Each team member also wanted to meet with David individually on a regular basis to discuss their own goals, targets and performance. David decided to meet formally with each of his six team members on a quarterly basis to do this.

Step 3 – performance evaluation

This is the formal, usually annual, performance review discussion between the manager and the individual about the individual's performance over the agreed review period. For this to be successful, both the manager and the individual need to be prepared. Each person needs to gather data and document information that will be useful in the performance evaluation discussion. A date for this discussion should be agreed upon well enough in advance to give both parties adequate time to do their preparation.

A proven and successful way to engage an individual in this step is to encourage them to undertake a self-assessment, where the person assesses their own performance against the agreed goals and targets. This ensures the individual will be focused on their own performance over the period and what they have or have not been able to achieve. It can be done using the organisation's own performance management documents (if they exist) or simply by listing the goals and the progress made for each.

The manager should also prepare information to be used in the discussion. It is the manager's commitment to this step that will send a strong message to the individual that the manager actually is interested in their performance and development. Useful and relevant information can come from:

- observation of the individual on the job
- feedback from clients, both internal and external
- feedback from peers, colleagues and others who interact with the person whilst they are doing the job
- sales results, reports and records that the organisation produces in relation to the results or outcomes of the business unit
- the previous year's performance review documentation, if it exists

As discussed in the previous chapter, the performance model can be used by the manager as a diagnostic tool to assist in their preparation for this meeting. It can be used as a mental map or checklist to help identify what is right, what is wrong and what is going on in a particular situation, with a specific individual. Just how to do this is the subject of the following chapters in this book.

Both parties should bring their preparation to the review discussion meeting so that it can be used as the basis of the discussion and guide the discussion's direction and content.

It is interesting to note that this formal performance evaluation step has been the subject of much debate, criticism and/or praise over the years. It has also been the subject of many courses, books and seminars for years and years. Although this is only one step in the whole performance management process, it is often the most disliked and difficult. It can also be the least productive if managers have not prepared adequately for the discussion or do not have the skills necessary to handle difficult or sensitive issues.

One of the outcomes of Wendy's performance review discussion was shared acknowledgment of her slowness in getting new proposals prepared. Her experience was extensive (25 years in the industry), but the discussion confirmed she was far from competent in some software packages she was required to use regularly in preparing proposals. The slowness was because she had to rely on others to help her in preparing parts of the proposal that had to be completed using the software packages.

Step 4 – corrective and adaptive action

An important outcome of the previous step is the identification of the individual's specific performance improvement and development needs. Once again, the manager and the individual should agree on a plan that will address these needs over the next 12 months or so.

The plan may include:

- attendance on specific training programs
- on-the-job training
- coaching by an 'expert'
- changing parts of the job description or clarifying 'roles'
- changing parts of the job
- participation in project teams
- provision of new or different tools, equipment or resources to enable the person to do their job better

- further clarification of job responsibilities, goals and targets
- a wider range of 'rewards'
- counselling, possibly about 'bigger picture' aspects of the role
- agreement to develop jointly a longer-term career plan to help the person achieve their career aspirations
- other actions designed to improve the individual's knowledge, skills, abilities and confidence

The plan may also involve the manager committing to address some aspect of the work environment in order to 'remove hurdles' or 'clear the way' for improved performance. It may also involve the manager recognising that in the future they need to provide more regular feedback or coaching to the individual. Or it may involve recognition by the individual that they need to seek more guidance or assistance when they have doubts or queries about the job.

By including any of the actions listed above, the plan implicitly addresses some or all of the relevant factors of the performance model. It will consider, for example:

- clarity of role
- competencies
- environmental factors
- values

Encouraging the individual to take an active part in the development of the plan and to take responsibility for organising some or all of the agreed actions will help the individual 'own' the plan. With the involvement of 'ownership', the individual is more likely to have a real interest in the plan being put into action and in achieving successful outcomes.

The recognition by Wendy and David that Wendy's computer software skills needed enhancement led to the development of a specific plan over the next few months. They agreed that Wendy would attend particular external PC software courses within the next four weeks. It was also agreed that one of her team members, Mohan, become a designated coach, someone in the office that Wendy could ask for assistance over the next two to three months until becoming fully competent on the software packages. Also, David agreed to follow up with Wendy after she completed the software course to check that the course provided the specific training she required.

After completing this step, the performance management process continues. The cycle is commenced again when the time is suitable, when it is time to set and agree goals and targets for the next review period.

This process of performance management, as outlined in Figure 3.2, can either be institutionalised in an organisation in a formal performance management system or it can be just the way an experienced and superior manager goes about managing the performance of their team members. When it is formalised, a manager is more likely to get support for the process from within the organisation. This can include the provision of documents such as forms for recording goals, targets and discussions and guidelines on what to do and when to do it. Some organisations also provide training on their performance management process and the performance management skills required by a manager. In fact, if such support is not made available, the likelihood of the system actually making a difference is much reduced. (Chapter 11 in this book identifies these skills and provides assistance on how to develop these skills.)

The progressive performance review

It is what happens, or does not happen, between each step that makes the whole performance management process a successful one or not. It is the essential action of providing regular feedback and coaching as an individual undertakes specific action to achieve their goals and targets that really makes the difference. Yet often this proves to be the most difficult step in the whole process. Figure 3.2 indicates that the manager should undertake this regular feedback throughout the whole performance management cycle, and not just at 'annual review' time!

One of the most effective ways to do this is to observe individuals in their own environment. Managers can observe, provide regular feedback and evaluate the individual's performance much more easily when they are amongst their workforce. In doing so, managers can reinforce the individual's goals and targets, provide both positive and constructive feedback and provide direction and/or assistance, on the spot, as required. In addition to improving the individual's performance, this behaviour by a manager can also lead to the building of trust between a manager and an individual and the development of an on-going, positive working relationship between the two.

Janet worked as an academic in a University. Students in her classes came from several different faculties. Janet had become very concerned over several years about the high failure rate in her subject. She had increasingly provided support material, mostly in printed form, for her students, but their continuing mediocre results had now left her questioning her own skills and abilities.

'Is the problem with me?' she asked her Head one day, during a long conversation about her classes. Janet was a highly committed lecturer, so they explored options with regard to getting some 'expert' evaluation of her work. Then Janet made it all very simple.

'Would you sit in on a couple of my classes, and provide me with some feedback?' she asked her Head. 'You may see some things I'm missing'. So that is what they agreed to do.

The important point is that the issue was discussed, and feedback was provided, at the time it was most needed, simply because the matter was talked about. Janet felt she was supported at a difficult time, and was getting some coaching, and the Head felt he had been able to help her adjust her performance and, at the same time, reinforce the trust in the relationship that was clearly underpinning it.

Many Australian organisations regularly undertake surveys of their staff to gauge staff satisfaction and morale and to identify specific issues that staff want addressed. One of the most common issues raised by staff in these surveys is their desire for increased feedback and coaching. So instead of just correcting staff or even criticising them, managers need to take a more active role in the day-to-day work of their staff. This does not mean 'looking over their shoulder' or following them around the workplace. It means being there to provide regular feedback, guidance and direction, to reinforce goals and targets and to build trust, just as described in the box above. The manager is there to coach individuals to come up with solutions to their problems and also to 'catch them doing something right'. One of the significant benefits of providing immediate feedback is that the individual is made aware of performance problems or mistakes as they occur, reducing the chance that the problem becomes an on-going one.

Think about your own organisation's performance management system (assuming there is one – if not, these questions are even more relevant!).

- How clear are the links between the corporate strategy, the business unit's objectives, and your own objectives?

- How significant is performance planning in the system? How much time do you devote to performance planning with each of your team members?

- How often do you have discussions with each team member about their progress against objectives?

- When and how do you formally evaluate performance? Do you include a self-assessment component?

- What follow-up is there to the formal performance review? How are performance improvement needs identified? How do you develop an improvement and development plan for or with someone?

Chapter 4

What's the job?
Role clarity

For people to perform well at work the most obvious and most important requirement is that they understand very clearly what their jobs involve. Without this understanding, mediocre performance is the very best that can be expected. Sounds simple. Of course we all know exactly what our work involves! Of course we know what is expected of us! Want to bet?

Try this as a simple check. Fill out the questionnaire on the next page. Then ask your boss to complete it focusing on your job. Then compare the two. It is always a useful experience and very often quite surprising when gaps in mutual understanding are revealed, as they usually are.

One study asked American Vice-Presidents and their subordinates to each define the subordinates' role. Of all the factors, or elements, of the role mentioned, there was only 35% agreement between the two people. Local research confirms that similar confusion about 'role' is alive and well here too!

My job, my role

Do this from memory. No referring to the filing cabinet or your PC files.

1. The four or five most important areas for me are (in order of importance):

   ....

   ....

2. The major outcomes required from my job are:

   ....

   ....

3. Targets (quantative where possible) which I am expected to meet are:

   ....

   ....

4. The most important people/departments for me to interact with are (in order of importance):

   ....

   ....

5. The individuals/groups over whom I have direct authority are:

   ....

   ....

A person's role is often defined by their job description, but in practice the role involves more than is found in a 'static' job description (which is often a year or two old, anyway). The person's role is created by the expectations of all those around them and with whom the person works and interacts. It is the result of what those others *expect* to be done and includes a shared understanding of the:

- performance goals
- targets
- key result areas and
- performance standards and measures

Some of these expectations, especially from bosses, will be reflected in job descriptions. Other expectations will be less visible but no less real. This is particularly so at middle and higher management levels. Job descriptions don't encompass the subtle and informal expectations that always exist. Every astute manager is aware that some of the most important aspects of the job remain unspoken. Furthermore, expectations change with time – role is a dynamic concept, not a static one.

Role confusion is easy – just recognise that for any person there are really three roles:

1. the role that *should* be performed
2. the role that the person *thinks* they are performing
3. the role that they are *actually* performing

and it is easy to understand how role conflict and role ambiguity flourish.

Setting objectives

A common method used to overcome these problems is to set objectives for a person's position. In practice, these tend to be restricted to the major achievements desired for the planning period. Such objectives usually aim to be:

- Clear – definite, specific and unambiguous
- Measurable – in terms of quantity and/or quality

- Consistent – with the desired end result of the organisation or operating unit
- Challenging – encouraging personal skills and knowledge growth
- Achievable – possible for the job holder to accomplish
- Acceptable – agreed to and accepted by both the person and their manager.

Objectives typically are made up of clear statements of what is to be done plus the standard. (Some people expect more of an objective: see Figure 4.1). Sometimes, objectives with clear standards are known as 'performance indicators'.

Role clarity is not merely a list of objectives, nor a job description. Consider the following: a high level of role clarity requires positive replies to these questions.

- Do I know what's expected of me?
- Do I know why it's expected?
- Do I know how I affect others?
- Do I know my sources of information/my expert advisers?
- Do I fully understand the unspoken (for example, dress code, social behaviours)?
- Do I know the limits of my authority and my behaviour? Do I know how elastic these are?
- Do I know, and accept, how much risk-taking is expected of me?
- Do I know where and how discussions are held which affect me?
- Do I know who my 'customers' are?
- Do I understand company policies and Code of Conduct?

What can the manager do?

Option 1 – create a job description

The most common step taken is to produce 'job descriptions' (or 'duty statements' or 'position descriptions'). They are particularly useful when the organisation is relatively stable and they therefore have a useful life in terms of time. In fast-changing organisations they can be outdated before they are distributed. They are also static by nature, time-bound and unable to communicate the subtleties. But they are still usually better than nothing. Just don't fall into the trap of believing that they are inviolate or a complete solution.

Some definitions

- Role ambiguity – is an individual's uncertainty as to what is supposed to be done. It arises from a person's misconceptions and is caused by a lack of definition of role.

- Role conflict – is the result of multiple demands being made of a person. It highlights uncertainty as to priorities: what should be done, when and for whom?

Option 2 – set objectives

Another common step is to set mutually agreed objectives. Because they specify outcomes they obviously help reduce ambiguities and conflict. The more widely each individual's objectives are understood, the more readily will role clarity be established. This objective-setting approach is described in Chapter 2 of this book.

These systems usually extend into performance management

Figure 4.1 What makes effective performance objectives? One view.

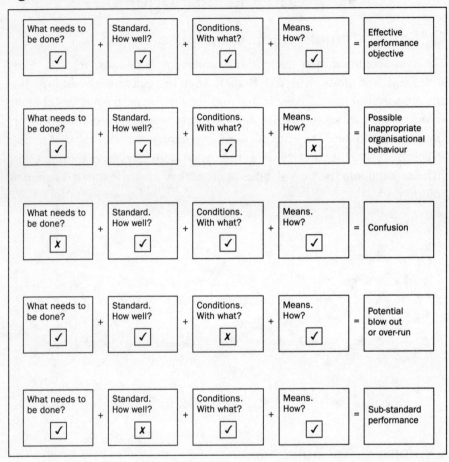

Source: Adapted from NIS Australia Pty Ltd (Brisbane) management training materials

procedures, which are the subject of Chapter 3 of this book. The regular review-coaching-development discussions that are a part of any effective performance management system can very significantly build role clarity between those involved in such discussions.

Option 3 – purposeful discussion

The regular performance review and development discussions referred to immediately above are far more useful in establishing role clarity than the paper-based appraisal systems which precede them.

So performance-related *purposeful conversations* are another way of clarifying roles. Don't dismiss it as too obvious and too simple. If such conversations are indeed obvious and simple, why do we find role clarity an issue in almost every organisation with which we work? It's clear that in practice these conversations don't occur often enough, if at all. Don't wait for the once-a-year appraisal routine to come around to trigger such a discussion. Managing performance is the fundamental responsibility of every manager, so discussions on performance, including role clarity issues, should be carried out as and when appropriate and certainly more frequently than once a year. Sounds easy? Kids' stuff? Yes, it is easy. No, it's not kids' stuff. Check it out for yourself, then set yourself a plan to improve it. Refer to Figure 3.2 in Chapter 3 to help you plan this.

CHECK

When did I last have a serious, detailed and honest conversation with my boss about the precise nature of my role?

When did I last have such a conversation with my own team members?

How confident am I that I understand fully my boss's role? (It is hard to work effectively with your boss if you are not clear about their role!)

Objective: I will set up role clarity discussions with:

Names:

-
-
-

On dates:

-
-
-

Particularly important aspects to discuss and clarify are:

-
-
-

The following is a report of a real problem:

It is a time of change – reinforced by the arrival of the new CEO.

One of the personnel changes was the promotion two months ago of Keith Gray, one of the Area Supervisors, to the position of Operations Manager. Although this was done fairly quickly, management were sure they had promoted the right person. However, now they're not so sure.

Stefan, the Head of Production Facilities, asked on Monday if Keith's computer had been down as he hadn't had any information from him since he took up the new job. Stefan depends on Keith; without his information he can't do his planning. A couple of other Section Heads have made similar complaints. The Branch Accountant was furious and was threatening to take the matter higher.

Now to cap it all off, Keith has not sent his Summary Report that was due last Friday. This was overlooked last month, when it was also late, to give Keith time to settle into his new role, but this is now the second month and still no report. The thing that puzzles everyone is that Keith is usually so conscientious; that's why he was promoted in the first place.

The situation was simply an example of lack of role clarity. No one had ever explained to Keith what was done with his Summary Report. When it was explained, Keith was apologetic and thereafter reported on time. A simple but purposeful performance-related conversation fixed what could have become a critical problem.

Option 4 – undertake a role-clarification exercise

Try a deliberate role-clarification exercise. One example of this is called *'Putting it on the table'*. The exercise is an extract from 'Putting it on the table', an interactive device produced by NIS Australia Pty Ltd (Brisbane) to assist in clarifying an individual's performance development needs. It is a matched pair of questionnaires designed to identify, among other things, areas where role clarity is lacking. The questionnaires are designed for separate completion by the person and by the manager or supervisor. The person answers for their job; the manager or supervisor answers for the same job.

A number of activities are listed in the first column and the person answers how important each is in their job. The manager does the same. They each use a 1–5 scale of importance and differences of opinion become very clear. (1 being most important, 5 being least important.)

'Putting it on the table' is also used to identify competency development needs. See Chapter 5.

'Putting it on the table' questionnaire

Activity	Importance in the job	How well implemented
Planning		
1. Setting realistic work targets		
2. Developing plans for jobs and projects		
3. Anticipating problems		
4. Managing work to achieve results within budget		

Activity	Importance in the job	How well implemented
Working with others		
5. Seeking feedback for self-improvement		
6. Listening to and understanding others' viewpoints		
7. Dealing with problem people and people problems		
Working with my boss		
8. Being responsive to requests and suggestions of my supervisor		
9. Proposing new ideas to my supervisor		
Managing people		
10. Providing development opportunities		
11. Giving clear directions		
12. Establishing performance standards		
13. Providing people with all the information they need to do the job		
14. Creating rewards		
Specific job skills		
15. Keeping up to date (knowledge)		
16. Relevant software skills		
17. [add here as appropriate]		

The questions are part of an interactive process between the individual and the manager or supervisor. It is *not* a performance appraisal or review. It is a simple structure designed to help produce plans for individuals. The questions and the format are designed to explore two things: what jobs/tasks are important (and how important) – that's the second column; and how well the important tasks are being done – that's the third column.

Individuals rate the importance of each item relative to their job on a 1–5 scale. Their supervisor or manager separately does the same. Individuals then rate their level of skill, expertise or competence for each item on a 1–5 scale with their supervisor or manager again doing the same. A discussion of similarities and gaps provides the basis for a development plan for the individual.

Option 5 – exchange of views and needs

If you want a framework for getting to the real issues but don't have time or cannot obtain the full questionnaire above, or a similar device, try the statements below. This is a mutual exchange. If you're the boss, put your 'authority' to one side (as far as possible).

You are aiming at an honest exchange with lots of listening. Nobody has to do what is asked of them at this stage, but you can learn a great deal about the other's expectations just by listening. Negotiating how to close some of the gaps, or needs, that are revealed is a separate second stage.

Some statements for getting started

1. Something you would like more of from me (because it would be helpful to you) is:

   ....

   ....

2. Something you would like me to continue doing just as I do now (because it is valuable to you just the way it is) is:

....

....

3. Something you would like less of from me (because you don't need it as much, or it gets in the way) is:

....

....

4. Something you would like me to stop doing (because you don't need it at all, or it is just not helpful) is:

....

....

5. Something which you would like me to start offering or doing (because you would find it helpful) is:

....

....

This review can also be conducted the other way around, so the feedback becomes two-way. Indeed the queries above, from managers to their team-mates, would usually be preceded by a manager-led discussion of what the manager would like from the team member.

Following clarification of each other's views and needs, some kind of negotiation can occur so that roles are better defined. The minimal outcome is much improved understanding of each other's position. Improvements beyond that depend on the nature and success of the negotiation and the extent to which people are serious about improving performance by changing the balance of who does what and how: that is, by readjusting their roles.

Option 6 – contribution matrix

The same kind of approach suggested above (in Option 5) as a 'one-to-one' procedure can also be used with groups: it's called a contribution matrix. Group members identify the issues, concerns, project opportunities or problems that they see as important. These are listed down the left-hand side of the matrix, as below, with team members' names across the top. Each team member has one of these sheets.

Contribution matrix

Issues	Leo	Carol	Ravi	Maya	Chris
1.					
2.					
3.					
4.					

Each person then indicates the nature of their own contribution to the successful handling of each issue and how they see the contribution of the others. The workshop leader, if it is being done in a workshop or team-building context, focuses people on their contributions. Avoid getting involved with concepts of responsibility or accountability. That will only muddy the water. It is what members of the group are going to do (contribute) that matters.

Each person classifies the nature of their own contribution as:

A = imperative to success of the project
B = important
C = a 'blessing' or a minor support
– = no contribution at all

These gradings are intentionally broad. The completed individual matrix sheets are then collected and a summary sheet produced. This can be done on a whiteboard if it is a workshop setting. Whether workshop or not, the group needs to view the summary data collectively because discussions about the ambiguities will immediately follow.

The summary may look something like the following (for a four-person group, plus the manager):

Issues	Leo	Carol	Ravi	Maya	Chris
1. This group's input to the company's new webpage. *(Only the 1st issue is used in this illustration)*	AAABA	ACCCB	ABC-B	BBBBB	CCBB-
2.					
3.					
4.					

How is this interpreted? The group sees Leo's contribution (or role activity) as almost universally an imperative contribution. The one exception sees it as important. A few minutes' discussion would clarify the ambiguity.

Carol's contribution is seen more diversely (greater role confusion): one person sees it as an imperative, one important and three 'blessings'. Considerable discussion is probably necessary before clarity can be established.

Ravi is even worse off, with a still greater range of opinions about his activity. Obviously, without the clarification that this sharing of perceptions provides, the first issue would proceed amidst much confusion and conflict.

Maya's role seems clear. All agree that it's important. Chris's is confused. One person sees him not involved at all, while two others believe his contribution is important. Resolution required!

The same routine is followed on the other priority issues identified by the group. This is a simple but powerful tool for identifying where role clarity is confused within a work group. The matrix, giving the group and its manager a chance to resolve misconceptions, makes different views visible and public.

The outcome is better mutual understanding of roles, some reallocating of tasks where appropriate and better performance as a consequence.

Bill Kemplar was the Finance Director. At a management meeting, a contribution matrix was completed for a list of key result areas and future strategies. Bill indicated that he had a C contribution to the key result area, profit. All other managers felt Bill was an A contributor.

Heated debate followed. Bill made it clear he was responsible for accounting for profits, but in his opinion it was generated by others.

The core of this problem was a failure to spell out role. Bill had moved into the job from an accounting background. Conceptually, he hadn't recognised the treasury function as driven by him.

Bill now runs a successful treasury operation, as well as a competent accounting function.

Option 7 – talk with your team often

Talk with, not at, your people *frequently*. And listen to what is said (or suggested through body language). This simplest of statements is something which many managers find difficult to implement. Not everyone possesses good listening skills. Consciously building within yourself the ability to listen, really listen, pays excellent dividends. All too often, managers allow these performance conversations to be driven off their agenda by other urgent, but less important, matters. So create space for the vital activity of performance management each month, ensuring those conversations highlight positives as well as shortfalls.

> Performance conversations are among the most critical of a manager's NOT URGENT, BUT IMPORTANT items for attention

Apart from anything else, most of your team will appreciate knowing where they stand, and how your expectations are developing.

Working on establishing role clarity

Role clarity issues are not just the responsibility of managers. Team members can also initiate improvements. In fact, you can start working on it even before you start in your new job.

Anita, a very competent young 'temp' with experience as a personal assistant to senior managers in several organisations, describes here how she manages her own role clarity.

'It starts with the interview', says Anita. 'After all, how can you know you even want the job until you are clear about just what it involves?'

'So I take a prepared list of questions with me. Some of them would be about:
● Reporting lines, for my manager as well as myself
● The range of duties

- *Which minor or even trivial tasks are part of the job (such as mail collection, coffee making, running messages)*
- *Which are the upper limits of responsibility that may be encountered (for example replying to correspondence without it being referred back to my boss; extent to which I can make diary commitments, database adjustments; or involvement with highly confidential information, such as replies to government Ministers)*
- *Involvement in my manager's "personal" matters (such as doing personal banking, handling family messages)*
- *Who else, if anyone, can make requests of me? And in what situations?*

Then, if I am offered the position, and accept it, I will go through these questions again with my new manager on the first day . . . sometimes their ideas are a little different from those talked about at interview, and I need to be very clear about the boundaries of my role. If I am to be judged as competent, or better, my manager and I both really need to understand each other's expectations.

And I need to be persistent, too. It is really easy, when you are "temping", for little deviations to creep in . . . you know, my manager is away for a day or two, so I'm asked if I can assist somewhere else . . . then people start to think I can help out there all the time, and it gets very fuzzy, and I get resentful. So I need that role clarity, and so does my boss, so that we can support each other, and I can work on the priorities and minimise side-tracks.

The worst jobs are the ones where you never seem to know what you should be doing because your manager lets things change all the time. That's really frustrating.'

Chapter 5

Can I do it?
Competency

The previous chapter was about understanding the job, the role and the work outcomes required. This is a vital factor in managing performance, but it's only the first factor. Clearly, added to role clarity must be the ability to do the job. This is a result of a person's knowledge, skill and aptitude (ability to learn to do the job and other relevant personal characteristics).

The combination of job-relevant knowledge and skill is called *competence*. Competence is the capacity to do the job or task or work to a stated standard. Without the appropriate level of competence, performance cannot be delivered. 'Competence' and 'competencies' are terms currently much in vogue (for example, competency-based training) – we refer to these particular uses of the word later in the chapter.

People develop competence in their work in a variety of ways. The experience of growing up provides a great deal of knowledge about many things. So does experience on the job, at work. School more formally requires the gaining of particular categories of knowledge or 'subjects', for

example chemistry, English literature, mathematics. Our work organisations similarly encourage the gaining of knowledge. Initially this may be
through an induction program, or 'orientation', for new employees ('Our
organisation works like this because . . .', and 'The department to which you
belong, Mary, fits in like this . . .'. Note that in this latter statement also lies
the beginning of role clarity for Mary). Beyond induction programs lie other
company-initiated actions aimed at imparting knowledge. Basic on-the-job
training is an obvious example, although it may be targeting skills as much
as, if not more than, knowledge. Other programs aimed at helping
individuals and groups get to know more about certain topics also fit into
this knowledge category (for example, seminars on 'Market opportunities in
Vietnam' or 'What your employment contract means' or 'Your business and
e-business').

Competence, however, requires more than just knowledge. It also
requires that the relevant knowledge, however obtained, can be applied;
that is, skill needs to be added to knowledge. The appropriate skills for the
task, together with the relevant body of knowledge, produce the required
competence. Both are necessary. The knowledge, without the skills, clearly
leads to incompetence; the task does not get done to the required standard,
if indeed it gets done at all. Remember some of those teachers or lecturers
from your own education who clearly knew a great deal about their subject
but lacked the ability (skill) to communicate it effectively. Their
performance, though perhaps well-intentioned, was clearly unsatisfactory.

Managers and skills

Effective managers use many different skills:

- technical skills to manage things, such as information and numerical
  data
- cognitive (thinking) skills to manage ideas, such as strategies, plans
  and systems

- interpersonal skills to manage people, relationships and themselves
- administrative skills to manage processes and procedures

In each category managers use diagnostic skills to explore what's happening and why, and extension skills (or 'doing' skills) to help them behave effectively and get things done.

A senior manager, responsible for his own staff department of 16 people, had good 'strategic' skills. His management style was aggressive, but he was also one of the few in the senior group who could create a sense of mission and state it so that others could understand.

Although this ability was respected by his senior colleagues, he used it to score points at the expense of others present at meetings. Few senior colleagues liked him, and a noticeable lack of personal invitations to various informal corporate gatherings was just one outcome.

Despite his lack of interpersonal competence, his tough and dominant style kept his department safe and unchallenged through several years of structural change. This was no small achievement. Then he retired. An almost immediate response to the 'vacancy' from the senior management group, many of whom were still harbouring memories of earlier put-downs, was to recommend the merger of the department with another. The retired senior manager's lack of interpersonal skills meant there were no strong supporters of his department's work, and the arguments put forward by his staff had not been listened to by him, or passed by him to others for comment or support.

A competence imbalance (good strategic vision, but poor interpersonal competence) had played a large part in the demise of the department.

An option available to this manager, but one he did not implement, was to appoint a deputy with good interpersonal skills and use this person to improve the collaborative reputation of the department. The outcome may then have been different.

The writings of Daniel Goleman on 'Emotional Intelligence' (or 'EQ') since 1995 provide perspective on this broad field of relationships and their impact on personal and workplace experiences and on effective leadership.

Building competence at work

Ensuring that the appropriate people have the appropriate competency is clearly a major task in any organisation. (This is so obvious that it probably explains why competency-based training or CBT is such a popular issue.)

Approaches to building competence range from recruiting in the knowledge and skills needed (but are there enough of them out there, and is this approach affordable?), selecting as effectively as possible, and/or building competence through various training and development activities both in-house and external.

These approaches assume that the organisation, and in particular the manager who is recruiting, selecting, educating or training, knows what is wanted and can specify this need in more or less measurable terms. This is a big assumption. Considering the cost (including time) of training, education and development, something better than an assumption is needed.

First, the demands of the job in terms of knowledge and skill must be understood and a range of 'job analysis' tools are available to produce this information. A description of the standard required for task performance is an important element of this job analysis. The focus then needs to shift to the individual:

- Just what is the extent of the person's knowledge base?
- Precisely what are the person's skills?

Again, a range of tools and techniques can be used to explore these questions, the techniques usually carrying the label of 'skills audit'.

A skills audit produces:

- a description of the job and specified standards for 'output'
- a description of the skills and knowledge (competence) available, either for individuals or teams as appropriate
- a gap, where some needed competencies are not on the list of what is available, or the needed competencies are not present to the desired level

Note that this is essentially an embryonic training needs analysis, where training needs are being identified so that the gap can be filled. Training needs analysis uses a variety of methods to identify needs (for example, one-to-one interviews, group interviews, questionnaires) but the aim is essentially as described above.

Competency-based training

Because of the need to improve workforce skills (and so improve workplace productivity), approaches to industrial training based on necessary and defined competencies have recently become of great interest. This has led to common usage of the phrase 'competency-based training', often abbreviated to CBT. (Do not confuse this CBT with another popular CBT: computer-based training!)

Competency-based training focuses on training outcomes; it aims to have trainees perform to industry-specific or other standards and is less concerned with a person's achievements relative to others in the group. Traditional training often has fixed periods of time for learning, but produces variable outcomes. Some people progress quickly and do very well, others barely 'pass'. CBT, by focusing on meeting job-related, defined standards of achievement, uses varying training times to produce outcomes to standard. It acknowledges that people learn at different speeds and through different methods and builds this into the training procedures.

The National Training Authority is encouraging CBT systems in Australia by endorsing national competency standards as they are developed by industrial bodies. The two major elements required for endorsement will be:

1. Training aimed at producing competency in using defined skills to defined standards of minimum achievement (and under defined conditions) within various occupations.

2. Assessment of competency achieved and certification of that accomplishment.

The development of CBT is being encouraged by continuing productivity pressures and the renegotiating of enterprise agreements, which highlight the need for:

● competency standards to be described appropriately

● training to be included in job descriptions

● multi-skilling

● clearer career paths with training options identified at various points

Managers and competencies

Considerable research has been carried out in the managerial competency area, with the aim of identifying just what it is that makes managers effective. One framework identified in early research is shown in Figure 5.1, with specific competencies gathered into the appropriate competency 'clusters'.

An insight into the breadth and depth of current competency-based development frameworks is found in Figure 5.2

Some original work has also been done by some management educators in using a 'competencies' framework for the development of post-graduate management degree courses. This builds on the existing research base and focuses the learner's development on those particular competencies which are most likely to make a significant difference to their managerial

Figure 5.1 Managers and competencies

Competencies	Competency clusters
Diagnosing situations, establishing frameworks	Goal setting and managing action
Proactivity; taking action to achieve	
Efficiency focus; being results-orientated	
Awareness of interplay of power and status when influencing and working with others	
Managing group processes	Human resource management
Managing power and relationships	
Maintaining self-awareness	
Goal clarification	Directing others
Communicating, delegating, monitoring	
Conceptualising	Leadership
Identifying cause and effect; being logical	
Decisiveness	
Ability to inspire	
Presenting visions, agreements and decisions; community	
Self-control	Focus on self
Stamina and flexibility for handling change	
Being objective, avoiding prejudices	
Detailed knowledge of:	Specialised knowledge
● 'technical' and other aspects	
● the task; command of the facts	

Adapted from Boyatzis, R. *The Competent Manager*, Wiley, New York, 1982.

performance. An illustration of the educational logic and procedures underlying this approach is shown in Figure 5.3.

Figure 5.2 An Australian competency framework

AN AUSTRALIAN COMPETENCY FRAMEWORK

Public Service Education and Training Australia (PSETA) is the nationally-recognised body for the public administration areas of Commonwealth and State/Territory governments.

PSETA developed the Public Services Training Package which was endorsed by the Australian National Training Authority in November 1999. This endorsement expires in November 2002.

This competency-based training package is highly comprehensive, totaling over 200 units of competency. These are organised into eighteen key areas: four of these are public sector-specific, the fifth contains generalist competencies based on the National Generic Occupational Health and Safety Competency Standards, and a further thirteen Key Areas are specialisations, of which six are drawn from other training packages.

1. Ethics and Accountability	7. Regulatory
2. Legislation and Compliance	8. Procurement and Contract Management
3. Policy Implementation	9. Human Resources
4. Working in Government	10. Management
5. Occupational Health and Safety	11. Fraud Prevention, Detection, and Investigation
6. Policy Development	12. Project Management (Public)

An example of a unit is 'Uphold the Values and Principles of Public Service' under the Key Area of *'Ethics and Accountability'*. This unit covers the ethical conduct required of those in public service. The elements of this core competency are:

1. Apply ethical standards.
2. Deal with ethical problems.

Each of these elements has a number of performance criteria. Those listed for 'Deal with ethical problems' are:

- Situations which pose ethical problems are resolved or referred in accordance with organisational guidelines
- Decision-making processes used to resolve ethical problems are recorded in accordance with organisational policy and procedures
- Organisational policies/codes on the prevention and reporting of unethical conduct are accessed and applied.

Critical aspects of evidence of competency are:

- integrated demonstration of all elements and their related performance criteria
- knowledge of Commonwealth/State/Territory organisational values and codes of ethics/conduct
- knowledge of fundamental ethical principles and how these relate to the public sector
- evidence of ethical conduct in a range (2 or more) of generalist or specialist work activities, such as delivering client services, using financial resources, procuring goods or services

(Information drawn from Public Service Education and Training Australia Inc – http://www.pseta.com.au/html/psp99.html – and compiled by Open Learning Australia, an agency delivering training and assessment for the Public Services Training Package.)

Source: Ron Harper, Open Learning Australia

Figure 5.3 A competency-based approach to management education

A competency-based approach to management education

The School of Management at RMIT University offers a three year part-time 'Master of Business Leadership' to experienced professionals who want to further develop their management competencies.

Using various competency models as a starting point, the program takes each participating manager (student) through the following learning cycle:

1. Competency exploration

Introducing, practising and diagnosing competency strengths and weaknesses.

2. Learning objectives set (via learning contracts)

Developing a work-based action learning plan which focuses on intensive practice and conscious development of a particular competency.

3. Learning contract implementation (via action and reporting)

Over a period of 20 or so weeks, implementing the learning plan in the work environment. Experimenting 'consciously' with the competency and recording both the experience and learning outcomes in a learning journal.

4. Self, team and academic evaluation

Collecting and submitting evidence of learning outcomes to the 'learning team' (a group of five or six course colleagues who work together assisting each other's development over the three-year duration of the course) and to academic staff.

This learning contract cycle is emphasised in the first two years of the program. After repeating the cycle many times, participants have generated significant development of their management competencies and they have also learned to manage their own learning.

What can the manager do?

Any manager can make a significant start on exploring the competency of his or her team members by firstly sitting down, one-to-one, with each person and asking them just two questions.

The first is *'How important is this activity in your work?'* You ask the question already having your own opinion formed and so can compare your team member's answer with your own. And you can share this comparison with them, right there on the spot. You continue to ask this same question of many relevant activities, most of which may be planned by you and some (or many) of which may be offered by the team member. The answers and the resultant discussions about the similarities and differences in responses provide role clarity for the team member ('That's interesting, boss, I hadn't realised that activity "x" was seen as that important in the overall scheme of things.')

The second question of significance is *'How good are you at this activity?'* Again, the question is answered by both manager and team member as the question is successively asked of many different activities and the responses are shared as a starting point for discussion.

A major outcome is the identification of areas where competency levels are very good, adequate, or deficient; or more importantly, there is disagreement.

Conversations of this kind could, and should, occur in performance review and performance development discussions, but you don't have to wait until it is that time again or until someone else sends you the forms.

Secondly, managers can also seek other inputs into the competency of their team members through a number of other steps:

● observation of the person at work, 'on-the-job'

● feedback from those who interact with the team member regularly on the job, such as customers, clients, colleagues, peers

● new computer-based or internet-based forms of '360-degree feedback' ideally lead to the same kinds of conversations.

An example of these questions (*'How important . . .? How good . . .?'*) was shown in Chapter 4. Discussions arising from the responses identify needs and these can be met from a wide selection of competency-building options. Some of these will target quite specific skills. Others will build broader-based knowledge.

To summarise, competent managers:

● explore competencies as the need arises.

Competent managers also:

● ensure that plans are developed to address the deficiencies and that progress is monitored, regardless of how the data is originally gathered (electronic or otherwise);

● ensure that personal strengths are recognised.

Your imagination and your commitment to developing your people are probably bigger constraints than that good old excuse of 'no budget', or 'no time'. There are many valid approaches to improving competency. The following is not intended to be exhaustive; use it to build your own ideas.

● Look harder (again) at on-the-job training. Look especially at how much feedback your people receive on their level of competence. Feedback, appropriately delivered, is great encouragement for people to keep stretching their skills.

● Communicate clearly the 'big picture', where they fit in it, future trends and the implications for new knowledge and skills. This gives people understanding as to why on-going learning is important.

● Use some internal training programs, on-line or conventional. Include a requirement for on-the-job projects where new skills and insights are applied, following the training.

● Explore what could be achieved through an internal coaching system. Your HR people should be able to advise, or find out more.

● Use external courses and seminars. They may be short, long, evening, weekend, day, on-line, residential, in town or out of town. Check out what your Industry Association can offer. Look in the guidebooks at your local newsagency. Ask your HR people what's available. Ask the

universities. Ask local colleges. Ask the Australian Institute of
Management. Get on the Internet!

- Consider self-instructional programs. Personal computers are making
  these widely available and increasingly flexible (also helps your people
  pick up new PC skills).

- By this time it's probably clear that you need to know more about what is
  available. And not just for your managers and your high achievers.
  Support their attendance at degree and postgraduate level courses at
  tertiary institutions. Meaningful support can come by way of serious
  discussions about career aspirations and development goals. You can
  also support attendance at degree and postgraduate level courses at
  tertiary institutions. Alternatively, consider support in the form of
  payment for course-related books, or some corporate subscriptions to
  relevant business journals, or paying part or all of fees. To get your
  money back, negotiate with the relevant professor that instead of writing
  an essay, or analysing a case study, they do a project back at work and
  apply their knowledge that way. There is a good chance you will recoup
  the cost inside six months, but the learning will be applied well beyond
  that time scale. Others who see it happening will also learn.

- Set mutually agreed learning objectives. It might be as simple as a
  reading assignment, a visit to a local Trade Fair, reducing the time
  taken for a particular operation or joining a 'Researching e-business
  opportunities' group. The individual pursues their objective to an
  agreed schedule and then reviews with you. There are also
  opportunities here for small group work.

- Use 'mentors' from other parts of the organisation or from other levels
  in the hierarchy to provide new insights, guidance and encouragement.

- To build an understanding of other jobs and to help people learn other
  skills, perhaps with an eye to the future, consider:
  * Secondments to other departments or subsidiaries

* 'Special project' work (when it is serious and purposeful)
* Job rotation, but with care. Watch for preference fit implications (see Chapter 8)
* Job exchange, perhaps private to public sector or vice versa

● If you really want one of your team (or yourself) to learn something about a subject, organise for them to teach it to someone else or to a small group. It raises anxiety levels, but it's very effective in building learning.

The 'time' dilemma

Managers never have enough time. But remember the enormous benefits to be gained if you make sufficient time available to develop the competencies of your team members. It was that 'old-time' American multi-millionaire Frank W. Woolworth who said:

'I never got very far until I stopped imagining I had to do everything myself.'

So you really do need to have good, competent people on your team if you want to make yourself a success!

Chapter 6

What do I do it with? The environment

The two previous chapters have looked at the issues of understanding the job (role clarity) and ability to do the job (competence).

As the model makes clear, these alone are insufficient for top performance. Even perfect role clarity, together with triple A competence, will not generate performance if a person has no tools with which to work. Or if there are too few colleagues with whom to share the job, or if an adequate number of helpers lack a common language, or if the system which brings components or resources to the workstation breaks down or is poorly designed, or if the server is down, or if leadership is deficient. Or if . . .

All these things will adversely affect performance. They are all part of the work environment, and they all need to be managed. The key question is 'Does the environment enable the job to be done?' That is, does it provide the person with the technical and human support needed, and are appropriate structures, reporting relationships and systems in place to enable the person to perform? These questions point to three major sub-environments which are examined in this chapter. They are:

1. The physical environment – including tools, technological aids and physical conditions.

2. The human environment – including peers, team members, others with whom the person relates, levels of compatibility and cohesion, and the quality and nature of the leadership.

3. The organisational environment – that is, the structure of the organisation and its sub-units, and the systems and procedures which it imposes on work activity.

These represent the resources available, but they also represent constraints. In addition there is a 'non-work' environment containing the numerous, and often complex, personal aspects of life. There are families, finances, leisure interests, friends, alcohol, community concerns, personal health, drugs, egos and a host of other factors which obviously impact on performance at work. Mostly, these are seen to be outside the manager's sphere of influence, or, in the opinion of many people, outside the manager's right to intercede. We will not enter into the moral issues concerning when a manager should or shouldn't step into, for instance, an alcohol-related performance problem. Each situation is unique and managers stepping into such situations need to be well-informed, to tread carefully and to exercise a high degree of sensitivity. Because it is of little value to generalise about such diverse and individual situations, this 'non-work' area is not pursued further here.

The physical environment

Probably the most obvious elements here are the tools and equipment needed to do the job. They are the resources required, at least the physical resources.

Without a crowbar and a shovel, the digger of holes in the road cannot perform. And too small or too large a shovel will adversely affect productivity. So it's not just a question of 'tools or no tools'; it's a question of appropriateness. The tools need to be the best fit to the task if performance is to be optimal. Most managers are only too well aware of this need for 'fit'. Many have recurrent nightmares when they think of the software or the web page (the 'tool') that is supposed to be doing a job for them, but which was

Figure 6.1 The environments around work

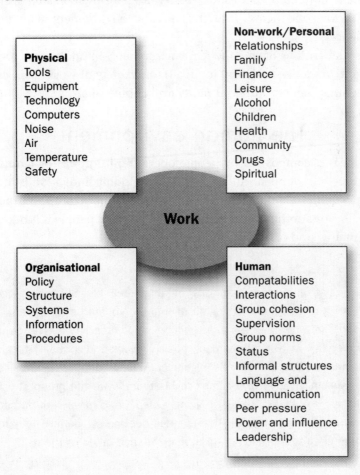

poorly specified or developed and which causes very significant performance shortfalls.

The crowbar and shovel can be replaced by other tools such as robots and computer aided manufacturing systems, but the principle remains. They need to be appropriate or performance at the individual level suffers. They also need to be cost-effective or performance at the corporate level suffers.

Further, poor equipment usually generates poor morale, so this environmental factor spills across into the 'human' environment with negative consequences.

Other dimensions of the physical environment, in addition to tools and equipment, are factors relating to 'health and safety at work' such as noise levels, lighting, temperature, humidity and quality of air.

The human environment

Most work is accomplished by people operating in groups or teams. Even where some jobs appear to be isolated or highly individualistic, those working in them still relate to others on either the 'input' or the 'output' side at some time or another. Clearly, interaction between people is fundamental to work in any kind of organisation.

> Quality initiatives are part of normal organisational life. But their success depends on creating the right kind of team, or human environment, and that in turn is a result of a manager's communication and listening skills.
>
> A supervisor in a local company, heavily involved in a quality program, found that it changed his role significantly, and required new skills of him – especially those of listening to his team. With the group structure established, and ideas flowing, he commented 'now I have all of my people really thinking – and they question me, and put up new ideas. The hardest thing has been to stop doing what I'm doing, and listen to them.'

But what is the nature of this interaction? What is its quality? How do I feel about working with Bill, Sean, Susan, Maria and Frans – and Ng who only started with us last week? He's pretty hard to understand a lot of the time. Then there's Werner, our supervisor: a good head for numbers and lots of technical experience, but sometimes not very confident about the bigger decisions.

Leaving the above individuals aside, what are the human factors that affect the way people perform in their jobs? Let's consider:

- the work group – colleagues, mates, peers, team members or just those who work 'at my level',
  and

- the leader, boss, supervisor or manager to whom the group looks for leadership.

Work group factors

These are many and varied. There are issues of compatibility, there are informal structures within groups, there are status differences, issues of cohesion, power, influence, aspects of communication and language, and the matter of peer pressure and the establishment of group norms, to name just a few. You could add other factors which you know are important in your own work groups. List some in the following table.

Human factors which influence the group environment in which I work
Group members are:
....
....

Positive influences: Negative influences:
....
....

Where do these factors originate? The starting point is in the 'individual differences' that characterise human beings. We are all just different. Call it 'personality' if you like, but looking behind that not very helpful label allows specific areas of difference to be identified.

People have different motives, objectives, needs, impulses, interests and values. This leads to them wanting different things. But they also have different beliefs: they think differently; they perceive, comprehend, process and conceptualise differently.

These differences are then reflected in behaviour. People act and react differently, signal their emotions and moods differently and so on. Given these individual differences as a starting point, it's hardly surprising that in a group setting, where many of the differences are on show, Sally doesn't always admire Bill's viewpoint and Charles is sometimes critical of Ruth's behaviour.

Group dynamics

This interplay of differences, even with the group focused on and committed to organisational goals, contributes to the dynamics of the group. A greater or lesser degree of cohesion develops, status differences emerge and group norms, or accepted ways of doing things, develop. If people accept each other, cohesion improves. If goals are widely accepted, there is better cohesion. If status differences are acceptable and norms agreed to, performance is more likely to increase.

Team roles

Another influence on the human environment is the interplay of a person's functional role contribution and actual team participation role. Some people are accountants, some engineers, some IT professionals, some marketers, and they contribute expertise from within these technical or professional roles. But there are other contributions needed by groups which are not related to these functional contributions. Groups also need objective setters, coordinators, ideas people, evaluators, information gatherers, team builders and good old-fashioned 'workers'. Having a leader is not a bad idea either.

These are not roles in which people achieve professional qualifications, such as the engineers and accountants and others hold, but they are roles which need to be filled if an effective team (and so an effective human environment) is to be developed. However, show us a group where three members concurrently aspire to the leader or chairperson role and we'll show you a group in conflict. Similarly, with too many clever ideas people, or too few (or no) producers, performance suffers as conflict between individuals gets in the way of task achievement or parts of the group's task fall into a hole.

Team roles important for team effectiveness

Considerable research (pioneered by Meredith Belbin, in the UK) indicates that some important team roles are:

- the chairperson who coordinates and controls
- the 'ideas person' or innovator who puts forward new ideas and novel solutions
- the 'producer' or 'implementor' who converts ideas to outcomes by developing plans and systems and puts in time and effort
- the 'shaper' or 'initiator' who sees opportunities, influences (shapes) team direction and focuses on action and results
- the 'evaluator' or inspector who analyses proposals, checks and makes judgments
- the 'contact person' who is usually hard to find because they are out searching for information, and building networks
- the 'mediator' who helps resolve conflicts, provides support and builds team spirit
- the 'specialist' who contributes mostly technical or professional expertise
- the 'completer' or 'finisher' who follows through, and manages deadlines

See R.M. Belbin for a description of early research in this field. An interesting extension of this 'team roles' concept is described in Figure 6.2.

Effective human environments acknowledge this and group members collectively work out their strengths or weaknesses as a way of clarifying who will do what.

Leadership factors

In addition to the impact on the human environment made by the group factors described above, the influence of the leader is obviously relevant. An effective leader sets the tone for the group, and much that has been described above takes place within this spoken or unspoken set of leader expectations. There is a strong likelihood of a person performing better as a group member if they have a positive view of the leader's behaviour. (For 'leader' in this context, read 'manager', 'section head', 'supervisor'.)

More has been written about leadership than almost any other topic in management and we are not going to try to summarise here the academic research conducted over the last century. But it is not hard to describe the major contributions that group members want from their leader. Most group members (not all, certainly, but most) value:

● A job made understandable to them, so they know what is required with minimal ambiguity, and an understanding of where they and their work colleagues fit in 'the big picture'.

  At the broadest level, it sounds like 'vision', which eventually reduces, for the individual, to 'role clarity'. It sounds like something a good leader would do.

● A chance to use the skills they possess, or to learn the skills required for effective performance.

  Sounds like 'competency' and, of course, a leader would provide the opportunity for skills use, and learning.

● A work environment where the technical resources and 'tools' are appropriate, where colleagues are reasonably compatible, and supportive and sensible systems and structures are in place. Also a boss

Figure 6.2 Team roles

Team roles

A different approach to team roles is used in proprietary material by NIS Australia (management trainers). In their approach, eight recognised team roles (down the left of the diagram below) are balanced by eight corresponding 'negative tendencies'. In the approach, a team role and a negative tendency are differentiated by an individual's preparedness to be a team member. For example, a person who enjoys handling quantitative data and willingly adopts a team role would most probably participate in the team activities as an examiner, checking things for the benefit of the team, while a second person who enjoys the same sort of data but isn't keen on playing a team role, may simply behave as a pedant.

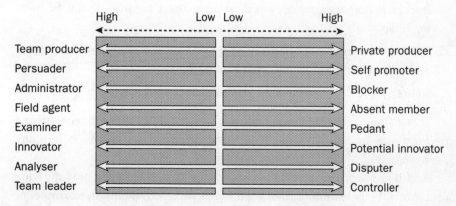

who knows what they are about, and provides both direction and support.

Sounds like a decent environment built by a leader.

- Being part of an organisation which they believe is doing something worthwhile, hopefully, but which is certainly not doing anything they see as wrong or inappropriate.

Sounds like a values fit, made clear by a leader.

● A chance to do what they most enjoy as part of the job, at least for a fair proportion of the time.

Sounds like preferences are substantially met, with a leader present to encourage this or to ensure that it happens.

● Rewards they see as fair, equitable and valued by them, in accordance with their motives and needs. The rewards will range from salary and favourable share purchase schemes, through fringe benefits, to opportunity to achieve, to a place in the team or in the limelight. Finding appropriate rewards and motivations is a 'horses for courses' business.

Sounds like the rewards factor in the performance model, and of course, good leaders do find appropriate reward opportunities. Otherwise, finally, followers stop following.

● Feedback on their performance, so they know how well they are doing and what they need to improve or develop.

Sounds like (and is) feedback, provided by an active leader.

This suggests that the leader should be working in accordance with the performance model. A leader's task and a manager's task is to manage performance.

And if you wanted to add that you'd also like to see your boss manage and motivate by example, then we'd agree with you. Being an example, or even being inspirational, is an important part of effective leadership.

Being an example

Leaders need to live by the same rules they expect their team members to observe. The leaders with real credibility are the ones who do just that. Leading is not a spectator sport. You can't lead from the stands, or from the corporate box, or from the bar, or the executive dining room, or from your well-furnished and comfortable office. You must do more than allude to strategy and provide support by just occasionally watching the game. But it is equally inappropriate to go out onto centre field and take on a player's role. The leader is there to create the determination and the strategy which will take the team to the top of the ladder. The leader is there to coach, to develop skills, to excite and develop the necessary belief and commitment. And in doing so they provide the ultimate example: they show others how to behave.

The organisational environment

So far we have looked at two important groups of factors in a person's immediate job environment: the tools, technology and other physical factors, plus the human influences coming from the work group itself and its leader. All of these, however, interact within a wider organisational setting: the structure of the organisation itself. This structure and the systems and procedures which flow from it also impact on the job environment. That is, the way work is broken down into different elements and the way in which reporting relationships are built so that coordination of effort and output can be achieved at minimal cost, affect performance.

This structure is the very backbone of an organisation and developing it so that there is an appropriate fit to the organisation's external environment and to its strategic objectives is of critical importance. Much of the change seen in both private and public sector life recently is aimed at changing structure so that organisations can continue to perform and remain competitive in a changing and increasingly deregulated world. That is, the new structure is a response to a new set of corporate goals, which are themselves a response to a changing environment. Those who have been involved in such changes know how difficult structural change can be and how performance is affected by the stresses and ambiguities which it produces.

Basic structures may be:

- functional – Production, R & D, Marketing, Admin/Finance, Staff Service groups
- geographic – a NSW, Vic, Qld, SA, WA or NZ business
- product – department stores versus supermarkets for Coles Myer, or trade books, textbooks and children's books for a publishing house
- customer – some banks have a retail, commercial and corporate structure
- divisional – where similar activities are grouped together under different divisional labels

Attempts at developing more flexibility, whilst still retaining effective coordination, have seen many hybrid structures emerge, and matrix structures are a further attempt to optimise the fit of the business and how it is organised to its external world. Increasingly, this challenge is to do with keeping parts of the organisation tightly structured, to achieve clarity and operating efficiency (and minimum cost), whilst allowing other parts of the business to stay loose and flexible in order to stay in touch with a changing external environment (despite higher costs of coordination and control).

Within this larger structural framework people pursue their tasks. For many people, the structure is a given. It's just 'there'. It may have been there, just as it is, for years (unlikely, these days!), or it may be changing. But if it is changing, those at lower levels are often unable to influence the change, so they cope as best they can. Again, implications for performance are clear.

What people are more aware of are the systems developed to control more finely the work of their particular section. These systems, which may provide people with raw materials or information, monitor quality, inform them of policy, pay them, provide feedback, direct their communications, all impact directly on what people do, how they do it and their resulting performance. Such systems contain detailed procedures, but whether it is the system or the procedure that impacts on the person in the job is not important. We just need to acknowledge that both, however labelled, have a major influence on individual performance.

> **85% of errors or waste are caused by systems faults, says Deming**
> TQM (Total Quality Management) is a popular concept and its application has been found valuable by many organisations. TQM success in western organisations is far from universal, although TQM principles are held responsible for much of Japan's industrial success in the last 40 or more years.
>
> A basic tenet of TQM is that error and waste and so poor productivity are mainly caused by poor systems. Dr W. Deming, one of the 'fathers' of TQM, claims 85% of errors or waste is due to systems faults, not employees' mistakes.
>
> Figures like that highlight the importance of systems in the performance arena.

Listen any night in any bar to a group of work mates talking. Much of it is light-hearted grizzling and much of it, for example, explaining 'why I've been messed around', is to do with inadequate systems. Some of it, true, will be focused on the innate stupidity of work mates (especially those from other departments), but if you look behind even those comments, it's often a 'system' inadequacy that is the real culprit.

So structure produces systems, systems produce procedures and they all have a very significant influence on how we all perform. When deficiencies are encountered, people become frustrated. They care less. They say the system won't let them work (and often it won't). The dangers are known to us all: structures that are top-heavy or too rigid, with tortuous communication paths; or systems which are overly complex, slow and obscuring the critical accountabilities; or procedures which become ends in themselves because the reasons for their existence have long since been forgotten.

One counterproductive system in a large professional services organisation grew from its concern for the security of its various buildings in the city. Security with regard to locking up buildings was strict and 'the system' proclaimed that buildings would remain locked on weekends. Many professional staff, who were wanting to work on some weekends, could not obtain access. Obviously, requests from senior managers for productivity, quality and excellence were met with derision. *'We'd like to be more productive'*, said staff, *'but we can't even get into the building outside normal hours to work voluntarily!'* Demotivation grew apace!

That administrative system was so well entrenched that it took more than a year to develop a weekend access routine that allowed staff to contribute as they wanted to!

If you, the manager, find these things downgrading performance, don't blame your people. It's not their fault. You are their chief. Go in to bat on their account; identify the causes, lobby for some support and take it up with your seniors. You are the manager and providing an environment which supports the kind of performance you need is your responsibility.

An organisation's environment and systems are constantly on view. You just have to look!

What can the manager do?

Managers can impact on all three 'environments'.

The physical environment

You are probably aware of much of the talk at work about the physical environment. Some of it will be good, some not so good. Why not explore this more thoroughly, for example, by auditing the adequacy of equipment? Or the difficulties of workplace layout? Why not make one of these issues a priority and ensure that something gets done about it. Soon. If you want to increase your own commitment to action, make a public statement to your group that you will fix it . . . and that you will do so within a certain time span.

Yes, there will be resource implications, but competent managers will not use this as an excuse. You can approach the issue simply by asking your team to consider their work environment priorities, to reject the fanciful and to develop an objective rationale to support a request for funds. You undertake to support the proposal to the very best of your ability.

You could review the most relevant health and safety standards and how they are communicated. For people to practise good standards, they need to know what is expected. Are the standards integrated with more recently developed quality improvement programs?

You could talk to the union and the HR group and the government agencies about health and safety at work issues. Their comments may give you valuable ideas for environmental improvement.

The human environment

Helping people to work together is basic to the job of managing. Perhaps the starting point is to ask people what is of concern either one-to-one, or in groups, or via a more formal questionnaire process. The actions you take will depend on the specific strengths and problems within your work group. Following are some possible actions to consider although this list is not exclusive.

Listening – again!

Listening occupies more of our working day than any other activity. It is widely quoted that we spend approximately 70% of our available time communicating.

Of that communicating time, many managers and supervisors spend approximately

10%   Writing or e-mailing
15%   Reading
30%   Talking
45%   Listening

This has long been recognised by nature, who always knew that listening was about twice as important as speaking. That's why we all have two ears, but only one mouth.

Team development activities

The human environment (call part of it 'morale' if you like) has much to do with how well teams perform. Take stock of your own team. Encourage team members to consider not only *what* they are working on (the task), but also *how* they work together (the process). To help focus discussion, you can use ready-made 'team effectiveness' rating scales, or you can create your own, which will be more relevant to the work in which you and your team are involved.

The team review questionnaire on page 92 illustrates one such diagnostic device. Its use involves team members scoring each statement on a simple scale (say 10 = terrific, we do that well, very good, or high; and 0 = dreadful; we do that poorly, very bad, or low). Each person does this as an individual and then the team pools their scores and discusses differences. Calculating an average and noting the range allows individuals to see where their views are supported by others and where they are not.

Subsequent discussions aimed at action, with action then being monitored, will often improve the team (human) environment very significantly. Discussions invariably touch upon who does what and how well it is done, so role clarity and competence come up for review as well.

There are numerous ways to address team-building. Books abound. Select one; make sure it is purposeful and related to the needs you have previously identified. At the very minimum, review the performance factors and identify which are the most relevant to teamwork.

Leadership

This is a vital element in the human environment. Leaders provide a vision of what might be; this differentiates them from managers (although a good manager is hopefully a leader). What can you do? How about starting with a self-audit (asking 'How well am I doing?') on the following leader/manager practices:

- **Creating the vision** and the longer-term goal (which will often imply changes), and communicating that vision in a way which infects others.

- **Clarifying roles** so others know where they fit, and what is expected of them, in the changing world of your vision.

- **Supporting others**, training them, developing them and acting as coach and mentor.

- **Involving others**, listening, really listening to their ideas, consulting with them and delegating meaningful and responsible tasks.

- **Communicating with and informing others**, so they know what is happening and can obtain the information they need to do well.

- **Goal setting**, defining standards, planning, organising and delegating, so all know what is to be done, why, how, when and where.

Team Review

As a team   Score /10
We have clear understanding of our goals   ☐
All are involved in setting goals   ☐
_____ (add your own   ☐
_____ additional items here)   ☐
                                                  ☐ sub-total

Inside the team
Leadership is well accepted   ☐
Communication works well   ☐
_____ (add your own   ☐
_____ additional items here)   ☐
                                                  ☐ sub-total

Among team members
Differences of opinion are addesssed openly   ☐
There's interest and concern for how well other   ☐
team members are doing
_____ (add your own   ☐
_____ additional items here)   ☐
                                                  ☐ sub-total

Team procedures
Meeting procedures work well   ☐
Decision making is effective   ☐
_____ (add your own   ☐
_____ additional items here)   ☐
                                                  ☐ sub-total

The team
Encourages creative ideas   ☐
Readily accepts necessary changes   ☐
_____ (add your own   ☐
_____ additional items here)   ☐
                                                  ☐ sub-total

Your team can calculate and discuss scores. We can't tell you what 'good' scores are for you and your team. But it's the discussion of the differences that helps teams develop and which improves the human environment. It's a journey, not a destination!

Source: Adapted from training materials of NIS Australia

- **Monitoring**, so you and others know how successfully goals are being met. Monitoring needs to be both internal, looking at operations, and external, looking at opportunities and threats in the business environment in which you operate.

- **Problem solving**, decision-making and 'fighting fires' (the fewer fires, the better!). Don't forget that decision-making is usually an excellent opportunity for offering involvement.

- **Networking** and finding information through a wide range of individuals.

- **Building your team** and constructively managing with them the conflict which is part of team and organisational life. Defending your team against others may be part of this.

- **Representing your group** both inside the organisation and outside it to other individuals, groups or organisations. This is an 'ambassadorial' or figurehead role.

- **Building commitment** via rewards and recognition, and motivating your team to stretch and see change as opportunity.

- **Being an example.** Are you doing it well enough and visibly enough so that your people aspire to your kind of judgment and behaviour?

Checking yourself against these practices will provide food for thought and stimulate ideas in areas that concern you. If you want feedback on some of these items, ask for it. You need some courage, but it's not as hard as you think; you have already covered some of it under the role clarity and competence discussions. Remember?

Performance appraisal discussions are usually a good opportunity to explore these leadership issues. Use the role clarity questions on pages 44 and 46 but with a leadership focus. Find out what your people's expectations are. Also make your expectations of them crystal clear: you will not achieve high performance levels unless you set high expectations.

Interpersonal skills

Much can be done by training individuals to improve interpersonal competencies. Included here could be development of conflict resolution practices, influencing skills, supportive communication skills, negotiating skills, sensitivity and collaborative problem solving. It can also be relevant to modify an individual's job to reduce interpersonal contact where it has disruptive consequences.

The organisational environment

The important factors here are the 'big' ones. The structure and its hierarchical implications, the authority system, the mainstream operating systems, the procedures, rules and prescribed communication pathways. All of them define and constrain what people do in their jobs. They are all supposed to make for smooth, efficient and effective operations overall, but it is not a perfect world. Murphy's Law is alive and well, and organisations at the best of times are complex creations operating in increasingly uncertain marketplaces. So it is not surprising that it is often hard going.

Getting all of the above factors 'right' and keeping them right over time (whatever we mean by 'right') is clearly not an easy task. But the attempt cannot be avoided. Without structure, an organisation cannot function at all: indeed these factors *are* the organisation, or at least its skeleton or framework.

The question remains: 'What can the manager do when this dimension of the 'environment' is constraining performance of individuals or teams?' The Chief Executive has the opportunity of changing these factors relatively quickly (given Board approval for some), but because of the fundamental nature of these environmental factors, the further down the organisation you live, the harder it is to bring about change. So the first suggestion is focus on what can (or might) be changed and do not use up a year's supply of nervous, innovative energy tackling the impossible.

Yes, that's difficult. Choosing what to challenge is walking a fine line; it is a question of your best judgment.

For short- to medium-term results look at what is getting in the way of doing today's business better. Where are the blockages? What needs to change? Ask your people these questions, if you haven't already. They will have lots to say.

For longer term results, aligned with a developing corporate strategy, it is more a matter of considering the 'fit': the fit of structure to strategy and to market trends; also the fit of the corporate strengths and weaknesses to the stated mission. These are top management issues, vital to long-term success and will be well examined in any corporate or strategic planning activity.

Coming back to 'performance' – there are many pathways to explore. They range from bringing in (if you have the authority) a team of consultants, through conducting a major organisational effectiveness review, to implementing better quality management systems, to setting up lower-level problem-solving teams, to setting up semi-autonomous and self-managing teams, to multi-skilling, to improved use of web pages, to *really* bringing the Internet into your business, to . . . on the list goes. Again, the strategic plan will provide a framework within which options can be shortlisted.

At the level of individual and team endeavour, and that's the level you can most readily influence, start by asking the team members themselves. They will know where blockages and constraints lie, just as you know where some lie. Develop your target list. Process it with your manager. They may be aware of good reasons why some apparent constraints are sensible and appropriate for the greater good. So your list may be reduced in size to issues that *are* worth tackling. Then it's into problem solving and planning for implementation of your solutions. Some of it may be easy. If it is, that's a lucky start. Mostly it won't be.

On page 98 is an organisational survey which may help you start. The better organisations in this first decade of the century will be the ones that start tackling all these performance issues now. The bad news is you don't have a choice. Good luck: it *will* make a difference.

Managers and leaders – some characteristics and some self-assessment

Here's a chance to assess some of your own leadership qualities

Leaders . . .	while others . . .	Leadership and me . . .	
		My own Rating	**Others rating of me**
Create positive visions of a new future	Talk about the need to survive		
Communicate that vision to others, and build their commitment to it	Demand 'commitment' because they are the boss		
Live their vision, and reinforce it by their actions and by example	Tell others what to do, and send them to communication courses		
Accept the accountability of making things happen – and then make some more things happen	Ask others 'what's happening?'		
Acknowledge responsible action carries risk, which they accept	Analyse and re-analyse and produce recommendations for others to consider		
Create new opportunities and new business	Maintain the status quo		

Leaders . . .	while others . . .	Leadership and me . . .	
		My own Rating	Others rating of me
Consider many mistakes as opportunities to learn	View all mistakes as punishable offences		
Make it easier for others to achieve goals – then ensure success is seen as the team's achievement	Push for results – and claim success as their own		
Are clear about their goals and their values	Are ambivalent and ambiguous about what matters most		
Catch their people doing something right and celebrate achievements	Manage by exception and offer only criticism to change behaviour		
Stay in touch by being out in the branches, the plant, the corridors, the marketplace	Stay in the office		
Manage their own career progression	Complain that the organisation is doing nothing for them		
Focus on doing the right things	Have a strong concern about doing things right		

Precise scoring is not required. Try:

AA for Almost Always	F for Frequently
HT for Half time	O for Occasionally
R for Rarely	then see how well others agree

Organisational survey

Answer the ten questions below for your organisation as a whole. Circle the number which represents your response.

4 Strongly agree
3 Agree
2 Neutral
1 Disagree
0 Strongly disagree
DK Do not know

1. We have a good track record of innovation by comparison with competitors in similar organisations	4	3	2	1	0	DK
2. Our management style does not impede the introduction and development of new products or processes	4	3	2	1	0	DK
3. In this organisation, the forces which favour the preservation of the status quo are balanced by enthusiasm	4	3	2	1	0	DK
4. It is generally accepted in the organisation that there is outstanding creative talent in its ranks	4	3	2	1	0	DK
5. There are influential people in the organisation who will support new ideas entirely on their merits	4	3	2	1	0	DK
6. The management control over activities is not an inhibiting factor for progress	4	3	2	1	0	DK

7. There are efficient mechanisms for the flow   4   3   2   1   0   DK
   of information necessary for managers to
   carry out their jobs

8. The organisation is attempting to stimulate   4   3   2   1   0   DK
   creative thinking through its training
   programs

9. Entrepreneurship is encouraged   4   3   2   1   0   DK

10. There is no feeling of defeatism where   4   3   2   1   0   DK
    new ideas are concerned

Source: Adapted from training material of NIS Australia Pty Ltd (Brisbane)

Total the scores from previous page here:

$$\underline{\hspace{1cm}} \times \frac{5}{2} = \hspace{0.5cm} \%$$

Identify the 3 or 4 highest scoring items. That is where your organisation is
strongest in managing for innovative performance. Low scores suggest
weaknesses or barriers. Identify the four (any four – high or low scores) which
you believe most need attention. List them below under 'Considerations' and
develop appropriate actions.

Considerations   Possible actions
....
....
....
....

Chapter 7

Is it right?
Values

The value systems that we each live by are deeply held beliefs, learned while we are young. We learn from our family, our peers, our schooling, our early religious exposure and from our experience. Sometimes we are directly taught values ('don't steal'). As we grow, we are influenced not just by our family, but also by the media, the law and by social convention.

A parent insists to a child, 'No, you're not going out with your friends on Friday evening. Grandma is coming for a family dinner and so are your cousins. It's a family night and you'll be there. These family gatherings are important'. This message, repeated to a young child in different ways, is very likely to result in a belief, carried on through life, that putting family first is a right and proper thing to do.

Other basic messages learned about what's right and what's wrong concern social behaviour, nationalism and environmental issues, to name just a few. These deeply held beliefs or convictions about basic rights and wrongs become a person's value system. Most of it is absorbed and established by the age of 10 or 12 years. People subsequently judge what they see and experience on the basis of this fundamental frame of reference. Changes in values, when they occur at all, occur only slowly. The simple illustration above, given significant reinforcement in the home, is likely to produce an adult who sees too much self-indulgent entertainment as wrong or at least undesirable and a strong commitment to family as right.

Organisational values

Not only individuals develop a set of values – work groups, teams, organisations, and institutions all develop their own set of values over time. Many factors can influence the development of organisational values:

- the vision and mission of the organisation
- the strategic goals and priorities of the organisation
- the values of the founders of the organisation
- the values of those leading the organisation
- the values of those making decisions within the organisation
- the external environment in which the organisation operates (for example, relevant competition, political, legislative and environmental factors)
- the financial position and strength of the organisation
- the visible behaviour of the senior management group, especially that of the CEO

In the organisational context, values can be explained by what the organisation stands for, by its boundaries for making decisions. Organisational values underpin the 'way things are done around here', the organisation's culture; they guide decision-making, business strategies, goals and priorities and employee behaviour. These values can either be explicitly stated (for example, in literature about the organisation, publicly displayed around the organisation, regularly communicated to and discussed with employees) or they can be implied (for example, by the way decisions are made, by what's deemed acceptable or unacceptable behaviour, by the priorities of the leaders and decision-makers).

Whether explicit or implied, these values are often referred to as the *core values* of the organisation. During the lifetime of an organisation, core values do not usually vary significantly. Unlike the strategic goals or the operational processes and systems of an organisation, the core values remain as the guiding principles for each successive management team in their drive for achieving on-going success and viability.

> Core values are '. . . *the organisation's essential and enduring tenets – a small set of general guiding principles; not to be confused with specific cultural or operating practices; not to be compromised for financial gain or short-term expediency* . . .' Collins & Porras (1997).

In organisations that have identified their core values and consider them critical to the organisation's overall success, the core values are often integrated into key management processes and systems. In this way, the values are simultaneously reflected in and reinforced by those processes and systems. For example, these values can be incorporated into such human resource management policies and processes such as:

- recruitment and selection
- induction of new employees
- identifying and rewarding performance
- promotion and transfer
- training and development
- pay and incentive systems

When the values are effectively filtered down through the organisation in this way, employees are more likely to reflect them in their own practice and behaviour. Without a values framework, it is very difficult to establish a common standard for leadership, decision-making and employee behaviour. Values provide a platform on which employees conduct business on behalf of the organisation and on which they make decisions.

Common examples of company core values:

- customer/client service
- quality service/products
- employee development
- teamwork
- integrity/honesty
- employee health and safety
- innovation
- accountability
- financial responsibility
- respect and care for the environment
- reward and recognition

Values and managing performance

What has all this got to do with managing performance? Simply (and importantly), there needs to be reasonable fit between a person's value system and the values recognised, reflected and practised by the employer organisation. Actually, it's the inverse of this that's most important. A good values match doesn't mean that someone will perform well above average. It just means that the person has no values-related reason not to perform.

What needs to be avoided is the situation where conflict exists between the individual's and the organisation's core values. In this situation, the individual does have a reason not to perform: they believe the job (or part of it) is 'wrong'. It contains activities or leads to outcomes that are opposed to the individual's values, so the individual does as little as possible in order to minimise the conflict (and guilt?) and performance falls away.

Charles is 54 years old. He joined the public sector organisation he now works for over 30 years ago. He knew that it (and sometimes he too) was seen as 'bureaucratic' but in the early days a concern for the community which it served was fairly widespread in the organisation. Charles liked that. Feeling he was doing something of broader value for the community was one of the reasons he didn't leave in the mid-1980s when pay was falling behind and friends said he should get out while he could. He didn't. Now, however, it's changing fast.

Concepts of fee-for-service are alive and well. And Charles, as part of his group, has been required to implement fees for their part of the service offered.

Charles believes it's just not right. He knows many who will be affected adversely although he acknowledges it will not be the most worrying issue in the lives of some of his clients. But it still sticks in his throat. He's talked about it a lot at coffee and lunch breaks and has thought very seriously about 'taking a stand' on it on more than one occasion. But he doesn't quite know how to do that and would it make a difference, he wonders? Work has not been enjoyable for Charles since all this began. The organisation he joined a long time ago is not what it was! He has lately taken to writing letters to the newspapers during office hours, just for a sense of doing something . . . but he feels it would be inadvisable to actually post one!

RESULT	– A performance problem!
DIAGNOSIS	– It is not role clarity. The role can be perfectly understood
	– It is not competence. All the needed knowledge and skills can be present
	– It is not environment. That can be fine
	– Values! This is the problem. And it's usually not an easy one to fix!

Clearly, Charles has a conflict of values. And it is negatively affecting his performance. What's happening to Charles is clear enough – his organisation is adopting a new strategy which is built upon a new, different value system. It is changing, as it must to survive. It is reflecting different values now and Charles is having trouble taking on these new values. The conflict is not great enough yet for Charles to quit, but it is certainly affecting his performance.

If this conflict is not recognised and addressed in some way, the ultimate outcome for Charles could be one of the following options:

1. Quit

2. Quit and stay

3. Stay and accept the new strategy

Obviously, for both Charles and his organisation, either 1 or 3 above would be preferable. In option 1, if Charles were to quit, the conflict for Charles would be removed and the organisation could recruit someone who was more in agreement with the new strategy (although Charles would have to find alternate employment and this may not be easy for him). For option 3 to occur, Charles' values conflict will need to be resolved and this would require significant understanding and communication between Charles and his manager.

But for both Charles and his organisation, option 2 is by far the worst outcome. 'Quit and stay' means that Charles will physically remain in the job but mentally and emotionally quit from his responsibilities and his commitment to the organisation. Neither Charles nor the organisation will win out of this outcome. In fact, both will lose. Charles will lose any job satisfaction that may remain and the organisation will have an unsatisfied, unmotivated and, possibly, a negative and even destructive employee whose performance will be well below par.

While the 'fee-for-service' aspect of the changes impacting on Charles will be clearly communicated within the organisation, the changing values which lie behind this may be far from explicit. Values are not always clearly and specifically communicated to employees. They are not usually signalled through memos or procedural statements – they are more commonly implied and spread by less formal methods, carried in anecdotes, stories and myths. Despite the 'softness' of the medium used, the clarity is there for those who pause and look behind the more visible actions of the organisations.

A similar sense of conflict was felt by Sally when the metals processing company she joined six years ago as a laboratory technician integrated backwards into mining. The lease the company had already obtained and the one they were negotiating, both in environmentally sensitive areas, had Sally and a few others at work expressing concerns and wondering about future developments. Sally was not as sure as she previously was that this was really where she wanted to build a career.

What's happening to Sally has not yet become as counter-productive as with Charles, but the warning signals are there.

A values gap

Clearly, a poor values match at least jeopardises, and finally reduces performance. And it is really nobody's fault. Changing environments, markets and competitive pressures cause organisations to change. They adapt by developing new and different strategies. And that is sensible. But in the process, some employees find that their new organisation is moving away from them, a values gap grows and they react adversely. Sometimes it is a passive semi-acceptance or even non-acceptance of the changed direction (that is, option 2 above), with performance falling to just sustainable minimal threshold levels or falling well below minimal threshold levels, respectively. Sometimes, the reaction can be active questioning or opposition to the change, which may also result in a 'quit and stay' response. Other times, when the conflict becomes too great and outweighs the benefits and security of remaining, people 'quit' and seek other work more compatible with their values.

A key indicator of alignment between an employee and the organisation is retention. Resignation from a position can indicate a values gap. It can be interpreted as a reduction in performance to zero. So this 'values' factor can, on occasion, be very significant in its effect! It is because of its overwhelming potential to impact so adversely, that it is placed in the equation (see page 19) as:

$$V \, (Pf \times Rw)$$

The V (for values) is outside the brackets to indicate it can pre-empt or overrule the other attitudinal factors of preferences and rewards.

Irrespective of employee's skills or qualifications, if they lack the necessary commitment to company values and strategic direction, they'll never perform to expectations.
Drake Executive Business Review, vol. 13, no. 2 (1999),
'Commitment: the Potential Downside'.

Imagine . . . you are offered a job by a friend of a friend. You don't know him well, barely at all, but the job sounds great. International travel every few months (you like that!) and mostly to South East Asia (one of your favourite places in the world!). Once there, you will be travelling inland, partly by light aircraft, well off the beaten track. It sounds like an adventure holiday of the kind you've always wanted (that's more 'strong fit' with your job preferences!). He even mentioned the possibility of some offshore sailing in coastal waters around northern Australia. 'How about rewards?' you ask. 'Don't worry' says this new boss. 'We'll start you with lots of money and build that into real sums over the first six months.' Terrific you think.

'What do I do?' you ask. 'Aha', says the boss. 'It's easy. You buy an air ticket to London but get off in Bangkok. Then you travel north, up into the Golden Triangle. Now at this village, you'll be met by my friends . . . they may look a little rough, but they'll be wanting to look after you very well. They'll give you a little case full of rice flour (well, it will look like rice flour!). You just bring that back here to me. Treat it carefully, it's worth lots . . . oh, and you needn't bother to tell Customs about it when you're coming through at the airport.'

Well, do you take the job of drug running? Probably not! The values conflict makes the other considerations of preference fit and reward, no matter how attractive they are, irrelevant, and you decline.

In this far-fetched example, $V = 0$. It is a total mismatch. So the job never gets started. Performance is zero. But in the opposite situation, where the match is very good, V would have an inferred value of 1. It doesn't multiply performance, or the $(Pf \times Rw)$ factor, because in this situation the job is seen as 'very OK'. But importantly, it does not detract where the match is good.

Managing your own values 'fit'

In the example above, more than likely, you would have consciously assessed the values associated with the 'job' and those of your new 'boss'. Realistically, when you are considering joining a new organisation, or when you are recruiting people to join your organisation, you should try to achieve a match between the different value sets. For example, if you are considering joining a new company, you should try to assess the organisation's values. Sometimes the values are explicitly stated as part of the interview process and you may even be given, during the recruitment process, company literature that, amongst other things, expresses the values of the organisation. You may find it helpful to ask customers of or those who interact with the organisation their opinions as to its values. Also, it would make sense to ask people in the organisation what they believe the organisation's values are in practice (as opposed to those publicly stated and espoused). By comparing the organisation's values with your own, you can evaluate how comfortably you would fit into the organisation. As explained previously in this chapter, a person will be most comfortable when there is a match between what is expected of you in the job, what you do, your values and the values of those around you, including the organisation's values.

Career mismatches

Career areas where mismatches are likely to be found in Australia currently are in those industries and organisations that are changing in quite basic ways, such as:

- scientific research and development (for example in regard to genetic engineering)
- education (especially tertiary, for example user pays)
- retail Banking

What are some of the basic values conflicts that may arise in these changing and developing industries?

In what other situations or industries do you see this occurring?

What is happening in your own organisation and how?

A reflection on your organisation's values

Does your organisation have a set of stated core values that underpin its vision and mission? If so, take some time to reflect on the questions below:

1. What are the organisation's core values?

2. What do these core values actually mean?

3. How do you actually demonstrate these values in what you do at work on a day-to-day basis, in your own decisions and actions?

4. What barriers get in the way of you demonstrating these values at work?

5. How do you expect your employees to demonstrate these values in their work on a day-to-day basis?

6. What are the things at work that actually encourage you and others to demonstrate these values?

What can the manager do?

Most managers will not encounter 'values issues' of such significance as in the fanciful drug-running example above; it is more likely that a manager will encounter issues like those affecting Charles or Sally. So what can the manager and the other people involved actually do?

As a manager, you are unlikely to change someone's value system and many would argue that you have no right to try. Sometimes, attempts are made by managers to 'buy' acceptance (by offering increased benefits, such as bonuses, salary, increased flexibility), but this does not reduce the moral concern and is unlikely to produce the kind of performance you want in the long run, anyway.

Recruitment and selection

Be aware of the need to make the organisation's current values known to an applicant during the recruitment and selection processes. If you are able to speak with confidence of the organisation's probable future direction and strategies, include these also. It may lead to a suitable candidate rejecting the job, but better that happens now, than after they have joined and found it to have been the wrong decision.

Don't be hesitant or apologetic about making the organisation's values public. This reduces the need for people to make assumptions about what the organisation's values are. Similarly, don't be hesitant to try to find out what are the candidate's values, too. You can do this by asking the candidate specific, behavioural-based questions during an interview, which will allow you to probe and identify where the candidate's values lie. This reduces the chance of selecting someone whose values do not match the organisation's values.

'Values'

An established, effective technique to help the interviewer obtain accurate information about a candidate's competencies (skills and knowledge) attitudes, values and traits and motives, is the use of specific behavioural-based questions. These questions are specifically tailored to the needs of the job and aim to identify what drives the candidate and what the candidate thinks, feels and wants to achieve in a job. Behavioural interview questions require a candidate to share their experiences in relation to specific situations – the candidate is asked to explain the circumstances of a specific situation, what they actually did, thought and said, and what the outcome of what the candidate did, thought and said was.

For example, to help determine if there is a match between a candidate's values and the organisation's values, the following questions could be used at interview:

1. If one of the organisation's core values is customer service, the interviewer could ask the candidate:

   'Tell me about a time when you displayed excellent customer service, for example, when you went out of your way to assist a customer' or

'Can you tell me about a time when you dealt with a difficult customer? What did you do and say? What was the outcome?'

2. For a core value of integrity/honesty, you could ask:

'Tell me about a time when you felt it necessary to go outside of or against company policy or procedures' or

'Tell me about a time when you stuck to company policy or procedures to solve a problem when it may have been easier or more efficient not to?'

3. For a core value of teamwork, you could ask:

'Tell me about a time when you put the goals of the team ahead of your personal goals' or

'Could you tell me about the most satisfying opportunity you have had recently to play a significant part in a team effort? What was your contribution? What was the outcome?'

4. For a core value of continuous improvement/quality, you could ask:

'Can you tell me about an idea you had about improving the way things are done at work? What led you to the idea and what did you do with it?'

'Tell me about a time when you were confronted with an unexpected problem. How did you deal with the problem? What was the outcome?'

For each of your organisation's core values, you can construct similar behavioural questions that will allow you to specifically probe the candidate about their own values.

A designer of integrated circuits had won its first defence contract. They had a history of very successful circuit design; no failures and always timely delivery. With the defence contract came problems. Design requirements did not seem to be that difficult but the chip designs were failing.

The team was small, so it was easy to determine each member's attitude to defence work. Some thought it was unfortunate that they had been required to work on such tasks, some did not mind working on them. Others disagreed with doing such work: they had been recruited to work on non-defence contracts. Once the value conflict was made clear, tasks could be better allocated based on values. The failures were subsequently minimised.

Organisational change

Be aware that change is a common catalyst of a values mismatch. Keeping team members and other stakeholders well informed before the change occurs maximises the chance they have to get used to the idea before it impacts on them. The downside of this is it also maximises the time available for them to organise resistance! Early involvement in the change issue and process is likely to reduce this resistance through increased sense of ownership. So communicate early and often and create opportunities for legitimate participation by those impacted by the change.

Counsel

Once you suspect a values 'gap', you need to confirm its existence and its adverse impact on performance. Once you have done this, you then at least need to raise it in a serious discussion with the person. This offers no guarantees, but it gets the issue out into the open and relieves the tension of what is often assumed to be a secret ('I mustn't let any one know I don't agree with what is happening or that I hold different views').

Effective counselling will help the person see the issue more accurately, often by providing more factual information. You are not likely to produce a shift in values, but by focusing on the issue rather than the person's position and clarifying the implications, the whole scenario may be seen in a more acceptable light. The person may then be able to 'live with the situation' rather than be in conflict with it through this better understanding.

Team building

Team building activities, whether in the form of team building seminars or workshops, team discussions or social interactions, offer a chance to solicit group views on what you know are sensitive or values-related issues with team members.

Apart from the chance of having the issue(s) better understood, those in the group who have concerns can hear the different views of their colleagues. The realisation is often reached:

(a) 'I'm not abnormal. Some others share similar views'.

(b) 'Those others who don't share my views and values are reasonable people, too . . . perhaps I could consider their positions a little more and maybe find ways of adjusting my own assumptions to an acceptable level.'

Make the values clear throughout the organisation

Looking at successful organisations around the world, it is evident that these organisations are more likely to have both a clear and well-understood vision and clear and well-understood core values. These together assist these organisations achieve their objectives. As a manager, you may not single-handedly be able to make the values clear throughout the whole organisation. However, you may be able to:

● communicate and model the core values in your own team

● provide on-the-job training and coaching to your team members which reinforce the core values

● encourage and work with your senior management team to define (or re-define), communicate and demonstrate the organisation's core values for all employees' understanding and benefit

The power of example

The Managing Director of a leading listed public company had initiated a cost-cutting drive.

One evening, following a University 'reunion' dinner, he said he'd drive an old friend, now living interstate, to his hotel. So they walked to the car park. The friend was surprised when the car's remote locking system flashed and revealed a Holden. A nice Holden, with leather seats and other nice touches, but a Holden.

'Where's the Mercedes?' the friend asked, thinking of an earlier visit that year.

'Ah', came the reply. 'It's gone. With the cost-cutting under way, I needed to set an example. But this one goes well'.

That is unusual Managing Director behaviour! The friend (yes, the writer!) should have taken the hint then and bought shares in his company – it's doing very well indeed!

Corporate values

The concern with corporate values is a long-standing one.

Twenty years ago, Peters and Waterman, who wrote *In Search of Excellence*, fame, confirmed that their 'excellent' companies were very clear on what their values were and equally, they took seriously the task of shaping and communicating those values. They (Peters and Waterman)

intimated that it was not possible to be an excellent company without clarity of values – and without values of the right kind.

Today, the same sentiments are again confirmed. The previously mentioned survey by Drake Consulting, involving almost 500 senior Australian executives, makes the same point . . . that high performing organisations ensure their values are visible, are widely shared and are adhered to at all levels of the company. Whether the values are 'of the right kind' or not, is a question that only time can decide.

Defining and articulating a company's core values

To do this effectively, an organisation really needs to go through a number of important steps:

1. Through consultation across the organisation, identify the organisation's current values

2. Determine if these current values are the desired values (that is, are they aligned with the organisation's vision and what it really stands for), once again, through consultation

3. Finalise and document the organisation's desired core values

4. For each core value, define actual behaviours that explain and underpin the value

5. Incorporate the values and behaviours into key human resource management strategies and processes, such as:
   - recruitment and selection
   - induction
   - performance management
   - recognition, reward and incentive
   - training and development

6. Regularly review the fit between the values, actual behaviours and management decisions, practices and actions

A recent survey of 500 senior Australian executives undertaken by Drake Consulting identified those key corporate values which the executives saw as important. At the top of this list were:

- customer/client service
- integrity, honesty and loyalty
- quality of product/service

The least frequently mentioned values are interesting . . . they were:

- growth and vision for the organisation
- financial responsibility
- reliable service delivery
- occupational health and safety
- valued and rewarded employees
- innovation

Clearly, governments wishing to foster innovation have a major task ahead of them!

The survey results are published in the *Drake Executive Review* (vol. 13, no. 2, 1999).

Chapter 8

Will I like it? Preference fit

While there is much academic debate about the causal relationship between job satisfaction and performance, there is little doubt that the two are related. It is common sense that people do well at jobs they like to do. The mechanic who works late to complete a job on a classic car, or the designer who forgets dinner and pushes on to create something new, or the writers who sit up late at night adding to the mountain of management books already available to you, are all valid examples of this pool.

Kable and Hicks' 'Decision Preference Analysis'

Research by Dr Jim Kable and Dr Richard Hicks (Kable, 1988) suggests that job satisfaction can be predicted from preference data. This research employed a measure of individual preference called DPA (Decision

Preference Analysis). This is a non-threatening questionnaire that asks a number of questions such as 'Would you rather study physics or design houses? Would you rather program a computer or interview people?' The answers are used to calculate a percentage score differentiating quantitative (QN) preferences from qualitative (QL) preferences. Conventionally, this percentage is presented as QN/QL and people with an 80/20 preference pattern, for example, have indicated they would prefer to spend 80% of their time on quantitative tasks and 20% on qualitative tasks. The extreme positions are:

80/20 highly quantitative (or QN)	An individual with this pattern will behave in a rational, sequential manner in a decision-making situation.
20/80 highly qualitative (or QL)	An individual with this pattern will behave in an intuitive, 'gut-feel' way in a decision-making situation.

Kable and Hicks also measured the QN/QL activity split in jobs. With several occupational groups they measured the job satisfaction of the people in the jobs, the QN/QL activity demand profiles of the jobs and the QN/QL personal preference profiles of the people. Their findings can be summarised as shown in Figure 8.1.

The DPA measures of both person and job have long been successfully applied. The personal profiles are virtually universally accepted ('Yes, that's me' is a common response). Recently, this measure has been further developed and updated, and presented as the Onetest Work Preference Profile. The Onetest Work Preference Profile has several significant improvements from the earlier DPA, not least of which is its presentation and availability via the internet (see www.onetest.com.au).

Figure 8.1 Job satisfaction and Preference 'fit'

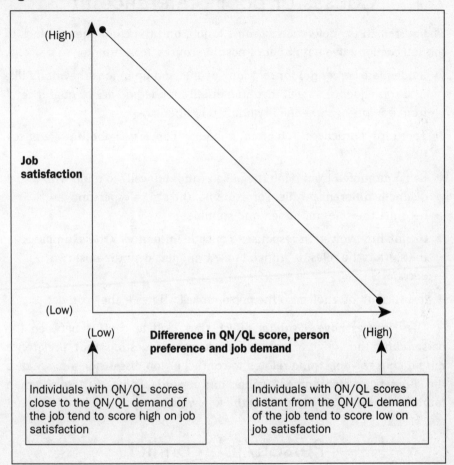

Causes of poor preference fit

The mismatch of preferences, people to job, and the consequential lack of job satisfaction have a number of possible causes, for example:

- inadequate career guidance. Many people end up in jobs they don't like as a consequence of well-meaning but ill-founded advice or guidance from parents or someone ill-qualified to offer it
- poor hiring practices. Too often, nobody is concerned about preference fit
- being promoted from a job they liked (and did well) to a job with a distinctly different profile. For example, the top salesperson who becomes the sales manager, and stumbles
- the job has evolved in response to outside influences. One example is the shift in the roles of branch bank managers over the past two decades
- insufficient job choice, so the person takes whatever they can get

These causes have a similar effect; they lead to conflict between the person and the job. We are not of course suggesting that preference mismatch is the *only* thing related to conflict or job dissatisfaction; see also the chapters on environment, values and rewards. Some of these common sources of conflict are explored in the following pages.

Person/job conflict

According to the DPA research, a person with a 30/70 profile would predictably be dissatisfied in a quantitative job (say 60/40). Certainly, there may be parts of the job they quite like, but overall there is likely to be dissatisfaction.

Look at the example of the DPA Personal Profile in Figure 8.2. The subject, F. Fillop, has a 30/70 profile. The subject also has particular scores

Figure 8.2 DPA Personal Profile

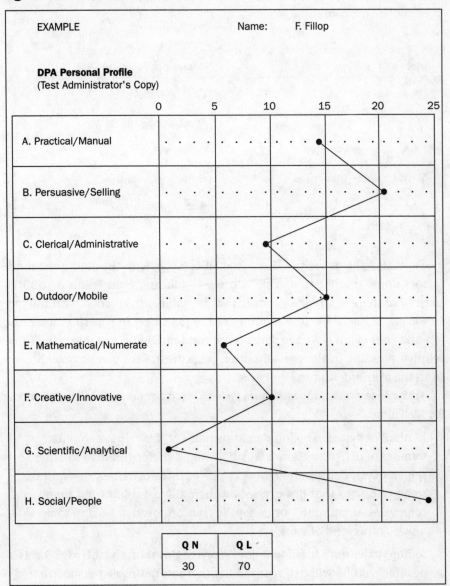

in eight preference factors which reveal the overall QN/QL score. These preference factors are:

Areas of preference	Areas of preference
QN sub-factors	QL sub-factors
Practical/manual	Persuasive/selling
Clerical/administrative	Outdoor/mobile
Mathematical/numerate	Creative/innovative
Scientific/analytical	Social/people

Figure 8.3 shows the profile of Fred Fillop's job, with the eight preference factors down the left side. This is a 60/40 job and Fred Fillop is a 30/70 person, so there is a high probably that he will be dissatisfied with the job. However, he might like the mobility of the job since, in this sub-factor, the job and Fred Fillop have the same score (and 'mobility' has much the same relative standing in the overall pattern of scores). This can be quickly seen from the overlaid data in Figure 8.4.

This overlay also suggests some specific areas of potential dissatisfaction for Mr Fillop:

● Manual activities. The job demands more of this relative to other families of activities than Fred Fillop would prefer (relative to other preferences). Perhaps he ignores some of these activities, delegates some (if he has that power), leaves them till last thing (and then complains of 'no time') or generally feels annoyed at having to do so much of this kind of work.

● Selling activities. Mr Fillop enjoys more of this than the job asks for. It is possible that he will get involved in other less desirable persuasive

Figure 8.3 Position Activity Profile (the job)

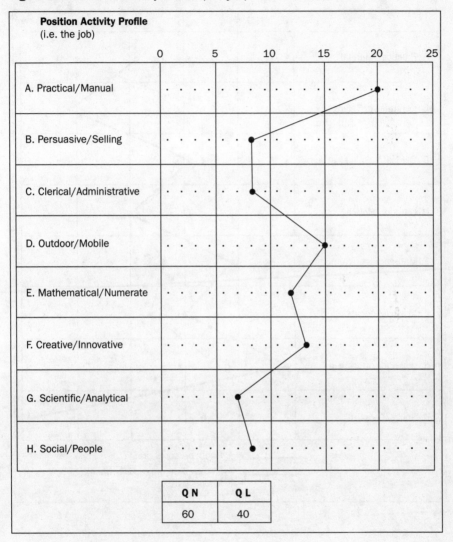

Figure 8.4 Overlaid data from Figures 8.2 and 8.3

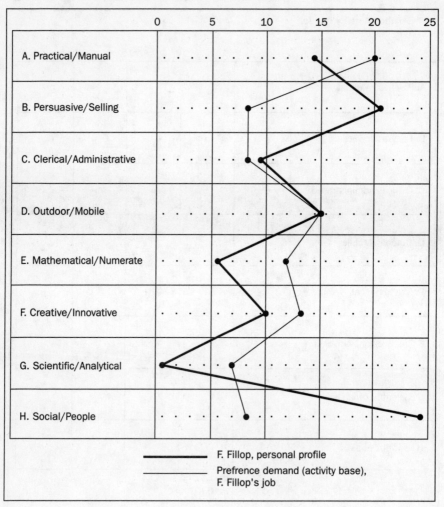

F. Fillop, personal profile
Prefrence demand (activity base),
F. Fillop's job

situations (such as office politics) or will find avenues for this preference outside work.

- Interpersonal (social/people) activities. Well, here's a real problem. Clearly, F Fillop is a highly people-oriented person, but the job is not. Even though Fillop may satisfy much of this outside of work, it's almost certain that we'll see evidence of Fillop getting involved in social interaction at work which could quite easily be interpreted as non-constructive. If his supervisor comments to that effect, then we can expect Fillop to show evidence of job dissatisfaction.

People in jobs which generally do not match their preference profiles will probably be dissatisfied, and their performance will be adversely affected.

The more modern Onetest Work Preference Profile takes a similar position in comparing a person to a position, and classifies the 'match' between the two as part of a report. The example at Figure 8.5 is classed as 'Very Well Matched' within the Onetest structure. Note that the Onetest Work Preference Profile uses the same eight preference factors, albeit with modified titles.

Person/person conflict

Can you imagine this conversation about stock levels?

Person A (70:30):	'How many have we got left?'
Person B (30:70):	'Plenty.' (A quite reasonable answer from a qualitative person to the question 'How many?' but probably totally disappointing to a quantitative questioner.)
A:	'Look, I need to know how many!'
B:	'I told you . . . there's no need to worry, we've got plenty.'
A:	'Are you dense? Just answer the question . . . how many?'

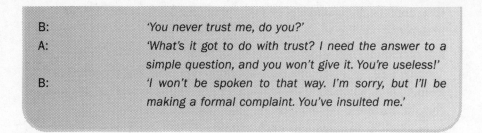

B:	'You never trust me, do you?'
A:	'What's it got to do with trust? I need the answer to a simple question, and you won't give it. You're useless!'
B:	'I won't be spoken to that way. I'm sorry, but I'll be making a formal complaint. You've insulted me.'

Figure 8.5 Example Onetest Work Preference Profile

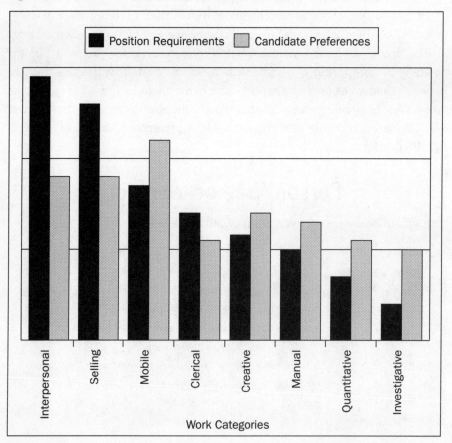

Not too unrealistic? It shouldn't be. It is based on an actual conversation. It's a simple example of how two people see the world differently, having a totally different frame of reference. Highly quantitative people see the world as something measurable, explainable. Highly qualitative people see the world as relationships, with lots of possibilities.

Of course, the conversation could be changed by having a team-like approach and introducing another person who has the ability to 'speak' in both ways, for example:

> Person A (70:30): 'How many have we got left?
>
> Person B (30:70): 'Plenty.'
>
> Person C (50:50): 'He means what number.'
>
> B: 'Oh, I see. Seventeen.'
>
> A: 'Thank you.'

Even the most qualitative of people would be able to respond quantitatively to the question, 'What number?' So if person A had asked it that way, the original conflict may have been averted. Being aware of our own preference profile and the profiles of those we work with can certainly help to minimise this type of interpersonal conflict.

> Person A (70:30): (I'm talking to a qualitative person, so I'll start less quantitatively, but try to give precise instructions when necessary.) 'How's the remaining stock look?'
>
> Person B (30:70): 'Good.' (He probably wants more than this . . . he's rather quantitative!) 'What do you need to know?'
>
> A: 'I need to record exactly how many we've got left.'
>
> B: (He probably means 'what number?') 'Seventeen.'
>
> A: 'Thank you.' (He's not that stupid if you ask the right question!)

This could be considered as part of the human environment (see Chapter 6). People working with other people who have distinctly different frames of reference will sometimes experience dissatisfaction and performance may suffer.

Try this. Think of three people at work. What are their major preference highs and lows? Remind yourself of the eight sub categories by referring to the earlier figures.

	Highs	Lows
Person 1.....................	....	....
Person 2.....................	....	....
Person 3.....................	....	....

What can the manager do?

As a manager of others, there is much in the preference fit area that you can take control of. Clearly, it is not possible to create a work-world in which everyone has a job that exactly suits their preferences. And nor would it necessarily be wise to so do. Some degree of dissatisfaction can be positive – for example, dissatisfaction which manifests as ambition might well be interpreted as a positive phenomenon. But it is possible to work towards a reasonable degree of job satisfaction for everyone. Shouldn't work be enjoyable?

Consider the following:

● Allow for differences in individual preference. Observe and attempt to allocate tasks on the basis of preference. For example, special projects can be deliberately given to those who show a relevant preference. A salesperson who has an unusual interest in mathematics might be the perfect choice for a novel market research project.

Nominate one person you know (..) who works in a particular position (..), but who has a specific preference (..) which could make them a potential choice for a project in ....

● Recognise opportunities for small modifications to jobs. Little changes can have big impact.

Robyn was a clerical worker in a pharmaceutical company. She seemed reasonably extroverted and certainly was 'people-oriented'. Her job unfortunately gave her little opportunity to mix with people and it was clear she felt the job was boring.

Her astute manager recognised the symptoms, and made organising briefings for doctors part of her job. This required a great deal of liaison and contact with venues, speakers and caterers. Robyn was saved as an employee and her clerical duties improved despite the time required for the new duties. She, quite simply, increased her productivity. Why? The job had become a much better fit with her preferences, so she liked it more.

● Counsel employees with direct reference to preferences. Preferences are important. People voluntarily leave jobs because they don't like them, not because they can't do them. Counsel before you lose talent. Such counselling can acknowledge that 'x' must be done, even though no one likes 'x'. But merely putting it on the table helps. Also, counselling sessions can touch on outside interests. Someone with a preference for outdoor and mobile type activity may recognise their own problems at work (if it is openly confronted) and be happy with suggestions for recreational activity outside of the work time. Preferences are whole-of-life phenomena, not just work phenomena.

● Training a person doesn't change that person's preferences, but it may certainly increase the person's efficiency in a particular area thus reducing time spent on the relevant activities. And less time spent on activity A might well allow more time on activity B, which could be important if A is not a preference and B is.

● Most people, but particularly the young, can benefit from a chance to discuss their career plans, or lack thereof, with someone in authority (and whether you view yourself as such, if you're 'the manager', then you are such). Too often, such discussions do not emphasise sufficiently the role of preference fit in terms of future job satisfaction. You can add this consideration to such discussions.

So there's quite a lot you can do. Just remain aware of preferences, just as you are already aware of people's competence. It's not hard.

Chapter 9

What's in it for me? Rewards

Each of us seems to find different situations rewarding. For example, one person goes home from a party saying, 'Wasn't that good. I met some interesting people', while a second says, 'What a bore. Trying to be polite to a bunch of strangers all night'. Or on returning from a serious bushwalk, one friend says, 'It felt good to climb to the top of that mountain', and the second says, 'I don't know. Seemed like a lot of hard work for little gain to me'.

Rewards are very personal. What each of us finds rewarding is, to a major extent, a consequence of our motivation.

Motivation is a difficult concept to describe. A starting point is to consider it as a driving force within the individual. Things that the individual needs, wants or desires may be regarded as positive forces urging the person towards some goal. Things that the individual fears or has an aversion to are generally perceived as negative forces that repel the individual away from a particular situation or set of conditions.

A tennis player who has a burning ambition to become a champion will exhibit dedicated behaviour that will take many forms. These might be typified by such things as endlessly practising, making enormous financial sacrifices, entering a seemingly endless series of tournaments and so on, all at great personal cost to self and family. That person is motivated. But if you were to ask that person about her motivation, she may or may not admit to possessing such an overwhelming ambition.

By comparison, another player may assert that she wants to become a champion, even though she does not act in a way that suggests that she will ever achieve that goal. Her behaviour suggests, in fact, that she is not as strongly motivated as the dedicated player and as such she is unlikely to succeed.

Behaviour is the best evidence we have regarding a person's motivation. The first player we mentioned will keep on working and trying until she ultimately becomes the champion or until a level of attainment is reached that provides her with the reward that she requires. This may also lead to widespread recognition and perhaps to the monetary gains that are usually associated with champion status.

Only when the reward is manifest and has become apparent can we start to recognise the motive, for at that point it is very clear that a need has been satisfied.

The concept of needs includes safety and comfort and involves both physiological and psychological drives. Drives tend to work hand-in-glove with rewards. If the rewards that are offered do not match up with the drives of the individual, then those particular rewards will fail to produce an urge to succeed. Since the reward is not perceived to be a reward, it fails to motivate. If drives exist without opportunities for a person to be rewarded, then that condition will simply lead to frustration or anger, and not to motivation.

In the case of our tennis player, that person had to learn that the result (achieving the championship and/or money) provided an intensely satisfying reward for her drive. If a general recognition of her superior performance failed to provide her with a reward, then she would never have persisted towards her goal. In other words, she would not have been motivated.

We learn what is rewarding. If you grew up in a typical middle-class family in Australia, you may have been exposed to a series of parental statements such as:

'Have you done your homework?'

'Yes.'

'Well, you can go out to play.'

or:

'No.'

'Well, you can't go out until you've finished.'

or another:

'Have you made your bed?'

'No.'

'Well, no TV for you.'

or:

'Yes.'

'Good. You can watch TV now.'

These patterns of reward and punishment are common with children. In the above examples, it is not difficult to see that the child is being taught to 'get things finished' and it is not difficult to imagine that, with enough reinforcement, the child may well learn to find all situations of 'getting things finished' to be rewarding.

Psychologists recognise a number of motives which are variously powerful for different people. Some of these are:

- achievement – the need to set clear targets and see results
- affiliation – the need to be with others, and/or help others
- power or status – the need to prevail over others (or be seen to)
- autonomy – the need for independence
- variety or novelty – the need to search out new ways to do things

It is not the list of motives which matters. In fact, good managers seem to be able to deliver appropriate rewards without any theoretical knowledge of motives. They deal with individual differences from observed behaviour. But it is important to recognise the wide range of things which people find rewarding.

Rewards at work seem to fall into two broad categories; there are those that are intrinsic to the work itself and those which are made explicit by managerial actions.

Intrinsic rewards come directly from the work. For example, someone with a strong affiliation motive would probably find a day of meeting people to be rewarding, but a day isolated in the back room to be 'demotivating'.

Explicit rewards are those the organisation and/or the manager make clear to the person, for example, the pay packet, recognition, an award or promotion.

There is some evidence that intrinsic rewards are at least as important as explicit rewards. Certainly, there is clear evidence of job dissatisfaction (and therefore poor performance) where a person's motives are not met by intrinsic rewards. Even if you offer someone a very high salary, if the work is not rewarding the salary may not be all that relevant. Rewards must be appropriate to motives. This has clear implications for job design and for managers who want to 'motivate'.

Tom was the Head of Engineering and Property in a major development company. Among other responsibilities he controlled a highly computerised drawing office consisting of a Senior Draftsman, four Drafting Officers and one Drafting Assistant.

For some time now he had been concerned that Sam Collard, the Senior Draftsman, was often hard to find when needed. Tom recognised that there was a need for Sam to visit various sections of the company as part of his work. However, there were a number of instances when Tom needed to speak to Sam urgently and had found him beside the coffee machine recounting his golfing prowess to another employee or sitting in a colleague's office giving an elongated description of his last fishing catch.

Twice in the last 12 months Tom has decided to deal firmly with this situation. On both occasions he spoke to Sam about the effects of his gregarious behaviour, while at the same time pointing out that his CAD work was excellent.

He can recall Sam muttering something about not getting enough time on the real job because of all the admin work he had to do'. Tom had been tempted to say 'Well, Sam, if you stayed at your workstation more you'd get it all done', but he didn't go that far. Instead he set some tight target deadlines for the ensuing week or two and in each case Sam responded positively and to his satisfaction. However, three or four weeks down the track, he was back to his old tricks.

Then, Sam's Drafting team came to Tom complaining that often they could not find their boss when they needed him.

Tom was forced to face the cause of Sam's performance shortfall. Sam was a person who needed affiliative reward, that is, frequent opportunity to meet and talk with others.

Once this was confronted, Tom and Sam were able to modify Sam's job, to make it more personally rewarding by building into it more opportunities for personal interaction.

Job design and modification, or what used to be called job enrichment, is an essential management activity. It is important for ensuring appropriateness of reward (the intrinsic aspects) and also for assisting in preference fit between person and job (see previous chapter).

Effective job modification is not necessarily a major job or task change. Sometimes very small modifications can give major gains. Encouraging a highly affiliative accountant to join a weekly sales meeting to discuss credit matters is a possible example. The change might be to only one hour in the week, but the incumbent now has an opportunity for human interaction which was previously not available.

It is interesting to speculate on why such workplace innovations as semi-autonomous groups or self-managed groups 'work'. It seems clear that the increased freedom (as well as responsibility) allows people to more frequently choose for themselves the more rewarding aspects of the work available, as well as to move towards a better fit of personal preferences to the job.

What can the manager do?

The following list makes clear that a range of rewards are available to managers, although not all rewards are available for use all of the time (for example, 'advancement' which is dependent on vacancies or opportunities, 'money' which is dependent on budget or a manager's discretion). Here are some things you can try.

Explicit rewards

Of course, there is money. But you should be able to acknowledge that not all explicit rewards are monetary.

- Money
- Assignment to a 'special project' (a meaningful one)
- Recognition – provided privately

- Recognition – provided publicly
- Increased control of key resources
- Symbols (the best PC, the biggest office, a car parking space)
- Promotion or advancement
- A chance to do more in the job of what you like best
- Time off
- More responsibility, more challenge
- Membership of a high-status group
- A chance to build valued skills
- Special duties (involving desired activities)

Remember too, that different contributions will be made by team members. Valued contributions warranting reward can be many and varied. For instance:

- Initiative
- Teamwork
- Clever, innovative solutions
- Decisive action
- Sound, persistent, non-spectacular, dogged work
- Vision or optimism
- Attention to detail and quality
- Foresight
- Loyalty
- Quiet effectiveness
- Instinctive leadership

The manager needs to decide which contributions are most important in a particular situation or job and offer rewards for those contributions.

Increased recognition

- Praise and provide other positive feedback when appropriate. This might include a congratulatory letter, a plaque, an 'award', a change in title, visible charts of progress
- Sharing of privileged information (for example, new business plans) with subordinates
- Seeking and responding to an employee's opinions on some issue which has important consequences on complex decision-making
- Invite to membership of a higher status group
- Status symbols, for example, car parking space or office decoration
- Representational roles on industry bodies

Increased development opportunities

- Sending to prestigious training programs
- Involving in meetings with the next tier management group
- Job rotation (if done carefully; consider preferences as in Chapter 8)
- International visit to associated organisations
- Hosting international visitors
- Organising role in social events (if appropriate)
- Membership of project team
- Internal secondment to e-business group or on-line development group

Increased responsibility

- Promotion
- Visible extension of authority
- New responsibilities/new duties. This is a rich field to explore with regard to internet opportunities
- Appointed temporary leader
- Budget expansion, provision of special funds

Implicit rewards

This is primarily an issue of job design or job enrichment. When designing jobs or modifying an existing job, acknowledge the needs and preferences of the incumbent or proposed incumbent. Build in where possible appropriate activities which will be rewarding to this person. We are all different, so allow for individual differences. You can offer 'reward x' to several people, but because of the differences that exist between them, some will value the reward more highly than others. The reward may inspire some to redouble their efforts but leave others unmoved. So don't expect identical reactions from everyone.

Goal setting – some considerations

When thinking about 'motivation', consider:

- Clearly defined goals are more likely to lead to higher performance than poorly expressed goals. 'Seven an hour' is clearer than 'as good as you can'.
- Goals which encourage stretching are more likely to lead to higher performance than easily reached targets, but even stretching goals must be attainable.
- Making goals visible helps to focus attention.
- Commitment to goals is essential for performance improvement. Commitment flows primarily from the expectation of success, which is a factor both of attainability of the goal and the history of goal attainment.
- A history of failure to reach goals can lead to an expectation of failure for even moderately stretching goals. Shortening the time period to demonstrate a pattern of goal-hitting can build expectation.
- Feedback can be as simple as a comparison of 'actual' to 'target'. Clear goals facilitate simple feedback, and feedback is essential in promoting performance.

● There is no simple 'best' way of expressing a goal. Goals should be
  appropriate to the motives of the person or group involved.

> Someone we know in a public sector organisation was once approached
> by her boss who suggested that she apply for an imminent vacancy at
> Departmental Head level. The person said 'I'm flattered, but no thank you',
> or something similar.
>
> 'You don't seem to understand', said the boss, 'this is a very significant
> career opportunity'.
>
> 'I'm sure it is', she said, 'but that's not the career path I want'.

The boss never did get to understand. The boss, to whom status was
important, saw himself bestowing a great opportunity (or reward). The
person who was approached valued autonomy highly, together with
the field work and client relationships her present job offered. She saw the
Departmental Head job as desk-bound and computer-tied, and the modest
salary increase just didn't compensate for that disincentive. So she declined.
She just didn't value the reward the boss thought he was offering. That is
'individual differences' at work, and you need to be aware of these
differences.

Chapter 10

Managing performance – what to do

In Chapters 2 and 3, two concepts were presented. One was the performance model (Figure 2.1) that a manager could use to:

- explain and understand the performance of team members
- diagnose apparent performance shortfalls or excesses
- address important factors in counselling and coaching
- agree performance improvement contracts with team members, and
- view people at work from a development perspective

The other was the performance management cycle (Figure 3.2).

An individual's 'performance plan' does not just happen nor come into existence as a result of a miraculous vision. Nor will it be provided by head office, the human resources department or your manager, if it is to be an effective plan. It will exist only as a result of hard work – work to clarify *what* and *how* the individual contributes to the organisation's goals and purpose, as part of performance planning. Similarly, a 'performance target' doesn't happen unless you set out to monitor and review performance. And this review doesn't lead to effective feedback and the development of new performance plans unless you evaluate performance.

The performance model (in Figure 2.1) is the link between 'evaluating performance' and the next step of 'corrective and adaptive action' (in Figure 3.2), and it is also a tool for use throughout this development process. This chapter is about how the performance factors can be considered during performance review discussions, feedback or coaching sessions.

Finding cause for performance shortfalls

When an individual's performance falls short, the cause needs to be known before corrective action can be taken. The cause may be:

- **An inappropriate performance plan**. Objectives which are set too high or are irrelevant could clearly lead to perceived unsatisfactory performance (see Chapters 2 and 3). Figure 10.1 is an example of a Performance Plan as part of a Performance Review document.

- **An unclear performance plan**. A lack of role clarity, confusion about priorities or purposes could have negative performance implications (see Chapter 4).

- **Lack of knowledge or capability**. The relationship of competence to performance is clear (see Chapter 5). Competence is a necessary pre-condition.

- **Inappropriate tools, equipment, work groups, leadership or other environmental constraints**. It is clearly difficult to do 'x' if the equipment needed for 'x' is not available, or if the work group is not functioning properly or if the systems or procedures are inadequate or inappropriate (see Chapter 6).

Figure 10.1 Your Key Result Areas

Key Result Areas relate to the major responsibility areas/objectives of your job. Each **Key Result Area** should be written as a brief description.

Key Result Areas should be consistent with and contribute to your team's and to the organisation's objectives.

Key Result Areas should be broken down into **Key Tasks**. **Also, Key Performance Indicators** should be identified for each **Key Result Area**. (Key Performance Indicators identify the standards or measures against which your performance will be assessed.)

Key Result Areas, Key Tasks and **Key Performance Indicators** should be discussed and agreed to at the start of the year by yourself and your manager. They should be regularly reviewed during the year, by you and your manager, to ensure each is still relevant and to monitor your progress.

Key Result Areas (What are the major responsibilities areas/objectives of your job? Refer to your Position Description)	Key Tasks (What major tasks are involved for each Key Result Area?)	Key Performance Indicators (How will you know if you have been successful in achieving each Key Result Area — what are the standards or measures for each?)

- **The task or action is not acceptable to the person**. Value conflicts do occur at work and people do withdraw their efforts, totally or partially, because of their individual concepts of 'what is right' (see Chapter 7).

- **The job includes tasks or responsibilities which the person does not like**. Preferences do affect application, effort and performance (see Chapter 8).

- **The job is so structured as to give too few intrinsic rewards appropriate to the person or their expectations of explicit rewards are not met** and the person simply has no incentive to try harder (see Chapter 9).

- **There has been insufficient or inappropriate feedback** throughout the year on all or some of the performance factors. The result is that the person does not know that more effort or different contributions are expected or that a shortfall exists. This will be covered in this chapter and is also referred to in Chapters 3 and 11.

Helping find cause is possibly the major use, in practice, of the performance model. It is a diagnostic tool, a checklist that provides a framework for performance diagnosis.

But the factors in the model can be also useful as a guide in performance feedback discussions. Diagnosis should not be a one-way street. Performance-related discussions, whether in a formal performance review/appraisal meeting or a more informal setting, should include a discussion of each factor and whether each factor represents strengths or areas to be worked on by *both* parties. We say both parties intentionally because effective development requires input from the manager as well as from the team member.

As stated in Chapter 3, traditional performance review discussions have a mixed record of success; evidence suggests that they are not easy to get right.

Performance appraisal reappraised

An article in the January/February 2000 edition of the *Harvard Business Review* (Grote, 2000) identifies a few innovative ways to evaluate performance. And much to the surprise of the article's author, these new methods are coming out of the American public sector.

The author, Dick Grote, writes that more and more organisations today are recognising that effective performance review is essential to the successful implementation of their strategies. Grote, in looking for 'best practice' in performance appraisal systems, has identified some fresh ideas for evaluating employees

One example he cites involves the US Air Force Laboratory in Ohio, which has refined its appraisal tool as result of recognised inadequacies. Of the 3,200 formal appraisals completed one year, not a single person had their performance rated as 'unsatisfactory' and only one person had theirs as 'marginal'. Not a reflection of reality, concludes Grote! The employees themselves were given the responsibility of designing a more effective system. The innovative system they developed is based on the value each job (and person) actually contributes to the organisation and each person's pay is a direct reflection of this. Quite a radical approach!

Another example describes how employees of the Minnesota Department of Transportation are assessed against what the employees themselves have identified and agreed as a 'true master' performer. Based on the organisation's mission and strategy, the employees identified the skills and behaviours they would need in order to successfully achieve the organisation's goals and objectives. Employees are now assessed as to how often they behave 'like the master' – occasionally, sometimes, frequently, providing a much improved, objective way to evaluate performance and give feedback.

Numerous factors affect how well formal performance review discussions proceed. Some of these are:

- **What is the manager hearing?** Their own opinion or that of the person being reviewed? Is the opinion based on fact or just a perception or hearsay? The feedback could be ill-informed and inaccurate, if the manager has a preconception as to why performance is unsatisfactory or why a particular behaviour has occurred. The manager needs to balance this preconception with fact and with the other person's view or with feedback from appropriate third parties (such as customers or clients).

- **The climate in the organisation.** Is the climate trusting, supportive and open or is it the opposite? Team members are more likely to rate the performance review as a useful process, meeting their development needs and goals in a trusting climate.

- **The review form.** Generally, review forms seem to help facilitate the discussion by providing a framework around which the discussion can take place. The forms should reflect what is important to the organisation, such as its values, performance goals and targets, and provide an opportunity for the person to include their self-appraisal and training and development plans. But it does not matter how good the form is, if, for example, it is used as an alternative to the discussion itself or the manager follows the form mechanically! In such cases, feedback would be totally unsatisfactory, impersonal and inefficient!

- **The person's job.** Jobs that are 'enriched' or seen as meaningful by the person doing the job lead to more constructive views of the performance review process. Perhaps this is because such jobs are themselves more likely to produce more feedback to the person doing the job, so that the review appears meaningful and relevant.

- **The manager's skills at conducting the review.** The manager's ability to provide constructive feedback, to encourage, to maintain self-esteem and to build trust and strong positive relationships clearly affect how both parties view the discussion. This is a vital consideration and many organisations' performance review systems remain ineffective because of insufficient skill development. (Chapter 11 addresses the skills required in providing feedback and conducting performance review discussions.)

- **Input from the person being reviewed** either before or during the discussion, leads to perceptions that work planning and development are the responsibility of both the manager and the person: so the person has a greater sense of ownership of the review. As mentioned in Chapter 3, seeking a self-appraisal from the person before the discussion impacts greatly on the ownership of the review.
- **Lack of structure to the feedback discussion**, that is, no simple and shared map. The form may provide a useful framework for the discussion and, of course, the performance model provides a checklist, which can act as a map or as a frame of reference for purposeful feedback.

The performance model and review discussions

Performance review discussions should, if they are to be effective, follow the 'map' and address the following points:

1. Results Achieved. That is, the **performance (P)** in the equation, which is the outcome of the interaction of all the other factors in the model. Has the person achieved the agreed goals and targets?

2. **Role clarity (Rc)**. Were the previously agreed objectives and tasks, standards and priorities achieved and other expectations regarding the purpose of the job fulfilled? Were they what both parties expected?

3. The adequacy of the person's skills and knowledge base or his or her competence, that is, the **competency** factor **(C)**.

4. The extent to which the physical environment, work group, structures, procedures and systems, together with the leader, support the work effort. That is, the **environment** factor **(E)**.

5. The fit between the organisation's values – reflected in its strategy,

direction and goals (which may be changing) – and the person's values and beliefs. That is, the **values (V)** in the model.

6. The extent to which the individual finds the work satisfying. That is, the **preference** factor **(Pf)**.

7. The appropriateness of rewards, both explicit and implicit, and their fit with the individual's needs, that is, the **reward** factor **(Rw)**.

8. The quality and relevance of **feedback**, which is the very purpose of the discussion in which these factors are explored.

Corrective and adaptive action and development

Any discussion covering the ground described will be comprehensive and will lead to a series of actions for the forthcoming period. This is about discussing and agreeing on what corrective and adaptive action is required to address any performance gaps. It is about putting in place a performance improvement plan. The significant aspect is that *you are not planning merely for results*. The plan focuses, instead, on some or all of the performance factors and should make clear who does what and by when, with regard to each of these factors. It has a real and significant development aspect to it.

This last point is important. The plan is not just for either the manager or the team member to implement: both have an important stake in the outcomes and both should be involved in its implementation and the monitoring of its implemenation in the forthcoming period.

The team member may accept an objective to master and incorporate into weekly work reports a new piece of software.

The manager may contract to organise the purchase and installation of the software. The manager may also contract to provide the time and resources for the person to attend training on the new software.

This 'contract', which is aimed at improved performance, may remain a verbal agreement between the manager and the person or, more appropriately, be written down as part of the performance review document. (Refer to Figure 10.2 for an example of a performance improvement plan, within a performance review form.) Either way, these performance planning outcomes have become a performance improvement plan. In drawing up a performance improvement plan, the focus of the performance review discussion shifts from discussion about past performance and outcomes, through diagnosis, to discussing and agreeing on the action to be taken, by both parties, during the period ahead.

Managing performance – a warning

Managing performance is a practical task. To do it well appropriate tools, as well as time, are needed.

Managing performance takes time. Often more of it than the manager feels able to give. But there is no alternative if the outcomes being sought, including the personal development outcomes, are to be achieved.

Planning to make this time available is a prerequisite for constructive results. Block out times in your diary for 'planning time', for speaking with those involved, such as the person, the people who interact with that person (such as clients, customers, peers), and for getting your thoughts and ideas in order.

Otherwise, your performance management 'system' becomes just another one of the many rituals that so many organisations impose, or allow to occur.

Yes – shortcutting it will save you *some* time. But the cost is that performance issues, which you know so well, will continue unchanged. And there is not much 'win-win' in that.

Performance Review systems are tools. And so is the performance model. Hopefully, the model can:

Figure 10.2 Performance improvement plan

This section is concerned with doing your current job better, in terms of both WHAT your job is (as outlined in Section 1 of this form — YOUR KEY RESULT AREAS) and HOW you do your job (as outlined in Section 2 of this form — THE ORGANISATION'S VALUES). It is also concerned with what training and development you need to achieve your longer-term career goals. It should be completed during your annual performance review discussion with your manager.

Identified Development Needs	Proposed Action to be taken to improve performance (which may include coaching, on-the-job assignments and/or training)	Action to be initiated by	Action to be completed by
WHAT – The Technical and Business Skills:			
HOW – The organisation's values, for example: • Customer Service • Integrity • Continuous Improvement • Consultation • Employee Development • Innovation			

- help identify the cause of performance shortfalls (or desirable excesses)
- make your feedback and coaching more productive
- establish meaningful contracts (performance plans) with team members
- provide a framework for the people doing the work to view it developmentally

These are fundamental to performance management and essential to making it happen.

Chapter 11

Managing performance – how to do it

In previous chapters, we have looked at what steps a manager needs to go through in the performance management process. We have also looked at the factors that influence individual performance at work and what can be done to identify and address the impact of these factors on performance.

This chapter aims to identify the skills required to do each of these essential tasks effectively. To optimise an individual's performance, a manager needs to be skilled at each of the following:

- Providing regular, constructive feedback – providing both negative and positive feedback on a regular basis

- Coaching – providing support, encouragement, feedback and training to assist a person to improve their skills and ultimately their overall performance.

- Conducting performance review discussions – identifying and addressing performance plans and together planning performance improvement strategies.

These are now examined in turn.

Providing feedback

One of the key skills in developing and maintaining good performance is giving feedback. When done well, it can help solve problems, reduce uncertainty, build positive working relationships, trust and effective teamwork and improve work quality.

Feedback, of course, can be both positive and negative. However, for most of us, giving negative feedback is much more difficult than giving positive feedback. We may feel that it is easier to ignore a problem and hope that it will disappear (particularly if we wait long enough!) but few real problems disappear by themselves. Not dealing with a problem when it happens may lead to the problem getting worse. Also, if we let unresolved problems or areas of concern build up, we may tend to explode when one more problem hits our desk. This can easily result in unnecessary (and unfair and unproductive) anger from the manager and also produce anger in the person concerned – a situation that may actually escalate the problem rather than solve it.

By not giving negative feedback when it is needed, a manager is not giving the person concerned the direction they need, nor does it help the person perform to the best of their ability. Negative feedback can help resolve isolated or on-going problems or recurring errors, help put a person's performance back on course and help deal with work or behaviour that does not meet the required standards.

Providing positive feedback, on the other hand, is usually easier to do and does not cause the same difficulties. Positive feedback is a fundamental element of regular communication between a manager and their team. It provides essential balance in communication about performance – if it were negative all the time, both parties would have little motivation to discuss performance and would probably work to avoid it completely!

To be of maximum value, feedback should be:

- intended to help the person to whom it is being given
- specific, rather than general
- given as soon as possible after the event that has triggered its need, while recognising that the receiver also needs to be ready to hear and accept it
- descriptive, rather than judgmental (that is, it describes facts, actions or behaviour and not the individual personally)
- focused on things the recipient can do something about
- given in a spirit of openness, co-operation and mutual give and take

The table below gives some examples of effective and ineffective feedback.

	NOT	BUT RATHER
Specific, not general	This work is full of errors.	The report lacks a summary, the main heading is off-centre and in a too small font and there are spelling mistakes throughout the text (and six in the first paragraph).
	What you did last week was great. Thanks.	When you stayed back last Tuesday, when you had to wait for the printer to be fixed, and completed your part of the project, it allowed the team to meet its deadline. Everyone in the team was very appreciative of what you did and we all benefited. Thanks.

	NOT	BUT RATHER
Descriptive, not judgmental	When you stupidly waste the company's money on short-sighted purchases . . .	When over 80% of your annual budget is spent in the first six months of the year . . .
	When you selfishly hide the key to the audio-visual room . . .	When you don't return the key to its proper place after you've used it, it causes problems for others.
Focus on what can be done or changed	I find your personality really impossible to deal with . . .	Your inability to complete work on time makes it very difficult for others – waiting for you to finish your work is causing delays for the whole team . . .

Steps in the feedback process

Providing feedback involves considerable well-planned and well-thought-out work by a manager. The following steps provide a framework for providing effective feedback. The feedback involved can be either positive or critical (negative) and, because providing negative feedback (on performance shortfalls) is more difficult, the focus below is on giving negative feedback *constructively*.

1. Preparation

The first step in giving constructive feedback is preparation; getting the facts and your ideas together before you talk with the person. You need to make sure that the purpose of your feedback is clear. You need to know what the issue really is and how you will describe it. Is it an aspect of the person's performance that is causing you concern and that needs to be improved? Is the purpose to share ideas about how to improve a particular process or procedure the person is involved in? Or is it about discussing inappropriate behaviour in the workplace?

To get to this point, you will need to have observed the person in action on the job, to have seen examples of the person's work, to have received specific feedback from others, such as customers, clients or colleagues, about the person's work or behaviour.

To be at this point, it is also assumed, of course, that you have made sure that your expectations about the job and how it is to be done and the person's expectations are in line. Expectations about what the job is and how it is to be done should be agreed at the beginning – when the person starts in the job or when the planning for the new year starts. It is too late to do this when you realise there is a performance problem. This has been discussed extensively in Chapters 3 and 10 in performance planning and goal setting. It is also part of the role clarity story in Chapter 4.

It may also help to prepare a script for the discussion ahead, at least to help you get started (scripting it all means you can't be listening). How will you open the discussion? What words will you use? Some suggestions include:

> *'I'd like to talk with you about . . . This is about . . . It seems to me that . . . I think we need to talk about . . . I'd like to get your ideas on how you think things are going'.*

A framework that often helps the feedback flow:

WHEN YOU . . . (describe the behaviour or action, factually)
THEN I . . . (describe your own reactions and feelings)
BECAUSE . . . (describe the outcome of their actions or behaviour)

This statement invites a response from the person and that usually opens the way for a discussion about the problem or issue and the way things could be improved.

2. Select the time and location

A golden rule for giving feedback is 'be timely and prompt'. Left too long after the event, the impact will be diminished – the apparent significance of the event will be decreased and the memory of the event may also have faded. However, if you are upset or angry about what has happened, then it's essential you calm down first. If the person is stressed, about to leave at the end of the day or upset about the event (or even something else), choose another time later. (But not too much later.)

Considering the location is also important. The more serious the feedback, then the more care should be taken in selecting the location. The key is to ensure that you will not be overheard or interrupted by others when giving the feedback. You need to be able to ensure confidentiality and security – this is essential in building trust and a strong relationship.

3. Providing the feedback

The next step is to conduct the discussion. A confident approach to providing the feedback helps set the scene – the following points will help you achieve this:

- Open the discussion honestly and get immediately to the point:
  - don't beat around the bush, state the purpose of the discussion immediately
  - come quickly to the point about the problem or the ineffective or inappropriate behaviour
  - don't bombard the person with questions
  - don't overwhelm the person with a flow of criticism
  - include recognition of positive and productive behaviour in other aspects of their job.
- Be specific about the actual circumstances of the problem or behaviour:
  - describe what you have observed or experienced
  - describe how the problem impacts on others (eg the team, customers)
  - don't use labels, such as sloppy, lazy

* concentrate on the problem and not on the person
* use the 'I' message technique, for example, 'I notice that you have been late for work three days this week. When you're late, other people have to take on your duties, customers are kept waiting and work piles up'.

● Seek the person's reaction to your feedback by giving them a chance to respond:
  * simply asking the person 'What do you think?' invites the person to provide their opinion and minimises them getting defensive. But having asked the question, stay quiet and listen!
  * encourage the person to ask you questions to clarify the situation
  * if the person denies the problem or behaviour, restate your position and the evidence you have.

● Ask for the person's suggestions on how the problem or behaviour could be solved or improved:
  * encourage the person to make their own suggestions for change and improvement
  * help the person maintain their self-esteem by genuinely seeking their input to the problem.

● Create a constructive environment for solving the problem:
  * help the person feel that you are providing the feedback so that a solution can be found (rather than just personally attacking the person or focusing on the problem)
  * take the initiative in suggesting improvements, if the person cannot do so
  * be specific about the changes you want to happen
  * probe what the person has to offer to solve the problem.

● Summarise the discussion and conclude with positive reinforcement of the person:
  * summarise what has been discussed and agreed about the person's performance and the action to be taken

* if relevant, provide positive feedback on the way the person has handled the feedback and thank them for their participation in the discussion and their ideas and willingness to address the problem or behaviour
* conclude with your belief that the person has the ability to do the job and to remedy the situation.

The points above focus on giving negative feedback to someone about a problem or behaviour. There will also be times, however, when you want to, and should, give positive feedback to a person about their performance. The keys to giving this kind of feedback are that it must be:

* genuine (if not true and sincere, your motives will be suspected and your credibility damaged)

* relevant to the person, their job and their performance

* balanced (that is, not over-the-top with praise or too gushy)

* given as the events dictate, as the person does something that deserves recognition and positive comment by you.

Since giving feedback is an ever-present aspect of effective performance management, mastering the skills required is worth the challenge. Increasingly, computer-based tools are available to help the manager meet this challenge. They are particularly helpful in gathering performance data. The recent, popular 360-degree feedback systems can be comprehensive and lead to time savings. They gather data from peers, subordinates, the manager and customers, and produce clear and detailed summaries. (See Topwheel website reference for an example.) They do not, of course, remove the need for feedback discussions.

Coaching

The role of a coach, at work and in other situations such as in sport or study, is to create an environment in which the people being coached can achieve optimum performance and, ultimately, their true potential. The idea is to *coach for success* – to take action *before* the person fails a set task or activity. When a person succeeds at a task or activity, their confidence builds and they become more receptive to taking on other, perhaps more challenging, tasks or activities.

To be an effective coach in the workplace, a manager needs to exhibit specific behaviours on a regular and consistent basis. These behaviours include:

- encouraging the self-esteem of the person being coached, by recognising their skills and abilities at present, their contribution to the team and the importance of their role in the organisation
- focusing on what effective behaviour and performance in the workplace is for them, helping the person identify their strengths and weaknesses, by encouraging their own self-assessment
- encouraging their participation by asking for assistance in problem-solving and decision-making and seeking their involvement in tasks and activities
- listening and responding to the person's ideas, issues and concerns
- giving regular constructive feedback
- encouraging them to take initiative in their work

By demonstrating these behaviours, you will help build a relationship that is a close partnership, one of mutual respect and trust and one that creates a positive environment, an environment for success.

Coaching – what is it and when should you do it?

Coaching is an active intervention by a manager to provide support, encouragement, feedback and training to assist an employee to improve their skills and their overall performance. It is the art of improving another person's performance.

Situations in the workplace that may require a manager to coach an employee include:

- inducting and training an employee new to the job and/or the organisation
- teaching a new skill to an employee
- explaining the standards and measures required in a job
- when an employee's work performance is below the required level
- when an employee needs help in sorting out what's important and what's not, what the priorities of the job are
- when an employee needs encouragement, needs to build their self-confidence
- when an employee is going to take on more challenging work
- when the organisation changes its strategy, its direction and its goals
- explaining the organisation's structure, its hierarchy, its politics, its culture, what behaviour is acceptable and what is not
- assisting an employee reach a level of performance that they have not achieved previously
- following up after any of the above.

Conducting performance review discussions

Performance review discussions are critical to an effective performance management process because this is when the manager formally meets with his or her employees to:

- review the employee's current responsibilities, goals and targets
- evaluate the employee's performance against these
- explore what both the person and the manager can do to ensure performance improvement

- agree on an action plan to address performance gaps
- review and agree on the employee's future goals and targets

These discussions play an integral role in any performance management system, as outlined in Chapters 3 and 10. Ideally, a performance review discussion should be a positive experience for both the person and the manager, but often they turn out to be stressful for both parties and may even be destructive.

Common sense tells us that some of the main reasons for failure in this step in a performance management program include:

- lack of adequate preparation
- giving subjective rather than objective feedback
- treating the review as a task to be done, rather than genuinely having the person's best interest at heart
- lack of skills and adequate training in conducting performance review discussions.

Similarly, as with providing regular constructive feedback (as described earlier in this chapter), there is a process for a manager to follow that will assist in conducting effective performance review discussions.

Preparation

1. Gather relevant information

The manager should gather all information that will be useful to the performance review discussion:

- consulting with other managers, clients, co-workers and customers, who have contact with the person in the performance of the job
- referring to previous performance review documents

- reviewing any current reports or job-related data relevant to the person's performance over the entire review period (and not just the most recent ones!)

This will help the manager assess how the person has progressed against agreed goals and targets.

2. Agree on a time and place well in advance

This will give both parties the time needed to prepare their thoughts and ideas and to gather the relevant information.

3. Involve the person in the process from the beginning

Ask the person to complete some form of self-appraisal, in which they assess their own performance against previously agreed goals and targets. In addition, encourage the person to review their achievements, think about their own development needs and short- and longer-term career aspirations.

The performance review discussion

1. Put the person at ease

Welcome the person to the discussion, making comments to build rapport and, perhaps, offering them a drink. The discussion should be held in a quiet, comfortable area, where you will not be overheard or interrupted.

2. Focus on the person's achievements, on the results achieved, on problems, on issues

Be specific in your comments, focusing the person's achievements during the review period first and then on the problems as problems (not as criticisms) and not on the employee's personality (refer to the section on giving specific feedback earlier in this chapter).

3. Explore causes with the person

Ask the person for their comments about their performance, about any problems or issues, about any obstacles or difficulties the person may have encountered during the review period. The person should be encouraged to talk, to ask questions, to add their comments and thoughts and to actively participate in the discussion. The person is then much more likely to feel satisfied with the discussion.

4. Listen

By demonstrating that you are willing to listen to the person, you will set the scene for an interactive and positive discussion. Communication experts recommend that, in these discussions, managers should listen up to 70% of the time, rather than dominate the discussion (as can be the natural tendency for some managers, particularly if they are anxious).

5. Explore options

Offer your own suggestions for ways the person can improve performance and ask for their suggestions on ways forward. Discuss these options, the pros and cons of each and the likely consequences of each.

6. Agree on goals, objectives and actions

The discussion should generate new goals and objectives to which both parties agree for the forthcoming period and actions to be taken by whom and when during that period.

7. Summarise the meeting and document what was discussed and agreed

Conclude the discussion by summarising what has been discussed and agreed. Also, you should indicate when you will complete the documentation of the discussion and give the person a copy for review and comment.

All performance review discussions should be conducted in such a way that both parties are clear on what has been discussed and agreed, and what action needs to be taken, by whom and when.

Using counselling techniques in performance review discussions

Experienced managers use, both consciously and unconsciously, techniques that help a staff member participate, contribute and feel a sense of ownership in a performance review discussion. These techniques include listening to the staff member's responses, objectives and ideas, acknowledging their reactions, feelings and emotions, addressing their concerns and showing empathy.

These are classic counselling techniques and can be listed as follows:

1. Encourage

2. Invite self-appraisal

3. Question

4. Observe the person's reactions

5. Reflect back to the person what the person has said or feels

6. Summarise

Using these techniques throughout a performance review discussion will assist a manager maintain the person's self-esteem, gain their involvement in the discussion and achieve clarity and understanding.

In addition to performance review discussions, these techniques can also be used in other complex or difficult discussions with employees (for example, handling conflict, introducing change, resolving problems).

It is not too difficult to describe what *should* occur (this chapter has done that). In reality, it is very challenging to do it well.

Practice is one of the keys

Another important aspect is to see performance management as a normal part of your role. Few managers, if any, are blessed with a team of 100% high performers. Performance shortfalls are the norm. If you can come to see the process of performance review as fundamental to managing, and participate in it with enthusiasm, you will do much to lift your team's performance, and your own levels of satisfaction and effectiveness.

Good teams can achieve unusual results. Sometimes extraordinary results. Manage your team's performance well and they, and you, can be one of the teams others talk about and seek to emulate.

References and further reading

Many general texts on 'Human Resource Management' (or similar titles) will include chapters on performance management.

Some more specific titles follow:

Bateman, M. (2000), 'Performance Management – the Hidden Dangers', *Training & Development in Australia*, Vol 27, No 3, June 2000, p.5.

Belbin, R.M. (1993), *Team Roles at Work*, Butterworth-Heinemann, Oxford.

Collins, J.C. & Porras, J.I. (1997), *Built to Last: Successful Habits of Visionary Companies*, Harper Business, New York.

Gill, C. (2000), 'Review Blues', *HR Monthly*, AHRI, August 2000, p.34.

Goleman, D. (1995), *Emotional Intelligence*, Bantam Books, New York.

Goleman, D. (1998), *Working with Emotional Intelligence*, Bloomsbury, London.

Grote, R. (2000), 'Performance Appraisal Reappraised', *Harvard Business Review*, Jan–Feb 2000, p.21.

Grote, R. (1996), *The Complete Guide to Performance Appraisal*, Amacom, New York.

Kable, J. (1988), *People, Preferences & Performance*, Wiley, Brisbane.

Lees, I. (1996), *Managing Performance and Goal Achievement*, McGraw Hill, Sydney.

Miltenyi, G. (1998), *360° Feedback Manual*, Business & Professional Publishing, Sydney.

Parker, W. and Matheson, S. (1999) 'Commitment: the Potential Downside'. *Drake Executive Review*, (Vol. 13, No. 2).

Peters, T.J. and Waterman R.H. (1982) *In Search of Excellence! Lessons from America's Best Run Companies*. New York: Harper & Row.

Pickett, L. (2000), 'People Make the Difference', *HR Monthly*, AHRI, May 2000, p.28.

Schaffer, R. (1991) 'Demand Better Results – and Get Them', *Harvard Business Review*, March–April.

Smither, J.W. (Ed) (1998), *Performance Appraisal: State of the Art in Practice*, Jossey-Bass, San Francisco.

Stone, R.J. (1998), *Human Resource Management*, Wiley (3rd Edn.), Brisbane.

Tornow, W.W., London, M. and CCL Associates (1998), *Maximising the Value of 360° Feedback*, Jossey-Bass, San Francisco.

Walton, J. (1999), *Strategic Human Resource Development*, Pearson Education, Sydney.

Websites

For performance management websites, go to www.google.com, and use 'performance management' as key words. Much will emerge!

www.onetest.com.au

www.topwheel.com.au

Index